HISTORIC INNS OF CALIFORNIA'S GOLD COUNTRY
COOKBOOK AND GUIDE

Published by:
Greater Success
Post Office Box 1616
Murphys, California 95247-1616
209/728-1616; 800/225-3764 extension 7
Fax: 209/728-1616

Edited by Joyce Mandeville
Printed and bound by Delta Lithographics, Valencia, California
Typesetting and graphics by 386Graphics, Dorrington, California

Cover Concept by Greater Success
Cover Art by 386Graphics

ISBN 0-9637112-0-2

The editor and publisher apologize but do not claim
responsibility for any errors or omissions

With Sincere Appreciation

This book is dedicated to all of you who have given us your encouragement and expertise during this project.

It is dedicated to the participating inns and wineries without whom this book could not have happened.

It is dedicated to our families (John, Amy, Ben, and Chas) who gave us tireless love as we moved forward.

And, most of all, this book is dedicated to our Lord Jesus Christ because of whom this dream has become a reality.

HISTORIC
INNS
OF
California's
Gold Country

COOKBOOK
& GUIDE

Welcome to California's Gold Country. The discovery of gold in 1848 changed California and America forever. Miners rushed in from around the globe, bringing with them a cosmopolitan air such as this sleepy little backwater area had never experienced. Most of the miners are long gone, but they left a legacy of fine food, warm hospitality, wonderful stories, and the history of a special part of the Golden State.

Our belief is that every meal should be a delight to the tongue; every bottle of wine is meant to be shared; and every story deserves to be heard.

Join us now for a bite to eat, a sip of foothill wine, and an exciting tour of the past and the present in...

California's Gold Country

Table of Contents

Map provided by California Department of Tourism

California's Gold Country ...At A Glance

This 300 mile long area was blessed with a vein of gold bearing quartz known to this day as the Mother Lode. Most of the Gold Country is conveniently located along the Golden Chain Highway 49, but treat your entire family by wandering the side roads and byways as you follow those argonauts of not so long ago.

Highway 49 begins in Sierra City, high in the Sierra Nevadas. It meanders down to Downieville, Grass Valley, and Nevada City. Well over a billion dollars in gold were taken from this one region alone.

The Highway will take you to Auburn to visit the oldest post office and volunteer fire department in the West. A short trip on Route 80 will take you to the Old Town area of Sacramento, California's State capital. Visit little Coloma where it all began at the site of Marshall Gold Discovery State Historic Park. 'Hangtown' a.k.a. Placerville, was rich in gold and figured in many tales of bad men and evil deeds.

Lovely Sutter Creek is a Victorian town filled with antique shops and historic delights. Farther down the chain, Jackson didn't lose its wild west image until the 1950s when the 'fancy ladies' finally took down their shingles.

Mokelumne Hill's buildings and ghost stories will take you back to the 1850s and San Andreas has kept Black Bart and the wild west alive all these years. A riverboat man from Missouri, Mark Twain, put Angels Camp and its frogs on the map for all time. A trip up Scenic Highway 4 will take you to the wine country of Murphys. Although a blanket was once sold in Murphys for five pounds of gold, prices have come down and you will love a leisurely visit along tree-lined Murphys Main Street.

Columbia is California's Williamsburg. A State Historic Park, Columbia is a trip back in time as you tour its 49er charm. Sonora, the Queen of the Southern Mines, is a bustling town that hasn't forgotten its early heyday. The Gold Rush never left Jamestown. Just outside of Jamestown you will find one of the world's biggest movie stars at Railtown 1897, a favorite location of Hollywood movie makers. Coulterville and Chinese Camp each offer their own bits of Gold Rush history.

After taking a side trip or two, Highway 49 will take you to Mariposa where you will find many well preserved buildings and other reminders of a golden past. The Golden Chain ends at Oakhurst, gateway to Yosemite, where 67 mines once operated.

Take your time as you tour California's Gold Country. Don't hesitate to take the road less traveled, risk getting lost, and finding out about the event that changed us all.

Photo from color print by Dick James

5

Sierra County Gold Country

Photo from color print by Dick James

Sierra County Gold Country

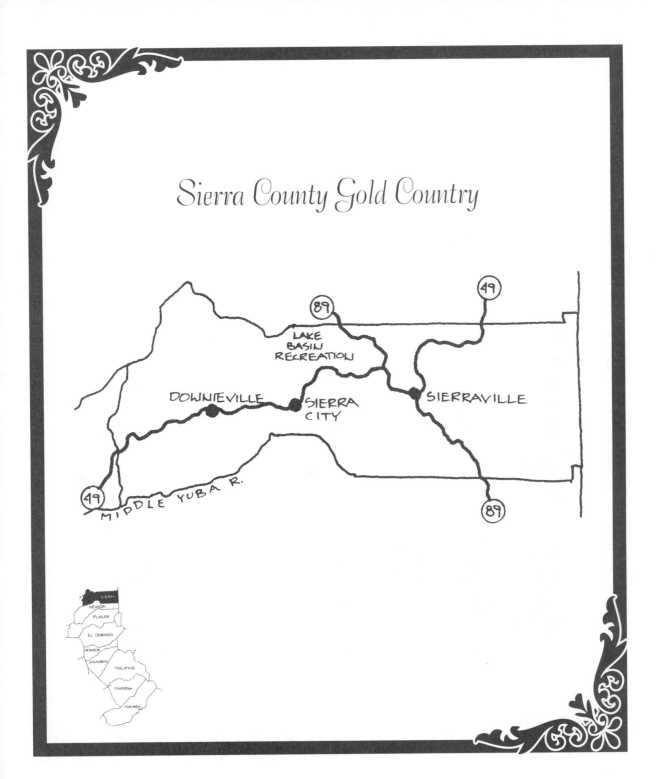

Sierra County

Sierra City

Sierra City sits at the top of the Golden Chain. The Sierra Buttes rise above this Gold Country town which was founded in 1850. The Sierra Butte Mine, producing over $17 million in gold, was opened by tunnels which led down to the Yuba River.

The notorious miner's fraternal order, E. Clampus Vitus, came into being in Sierra City. Some of the miners found the more conventional lodges and associations to be too tame and founded E. Clampus Vitus, which when translated means absolutely nothing. The members were pledged to informality, strong spirits, and high times, and ruled by a Noble Grand Humbug.

The Clampers were also known for a number of charitable acts, in spite of themselves. Their good works were always anonymous but a good reputation began to outweigh the bad. The Clampers died out along with the diggings but were revived in the 1930's. A number of historical markers erected by the society can be found in the region.

In spite of several natural disasters, many of the older buildings in Sierra City date from the 1860s, the largest of these being the Busch building which housed Wells Fargo in days gone by. The Zerloff Hotel was built in the 1860s and is still owned and operated by the same family. One mile east of town is the Kentucky Mine which has summer tours of the mine and stamp mill.

Behind the buttes, north of Sierra City, lies the pristine Gold Lakes area. Included in this string of alpine lakes is the little gem, Sardine Lake. Yes, you're right, sardines are a salt water fish. Sardine Lake was named for a mule named Sardine who drowned in the lake. Add this to the short list of lakes named for drowned mules.

Downieville

In 1849, William Downie of Scotland and several other men wintered at the fork of the Yuba and what would become the Downie Rivers. A salmon was caught, cooked, and consumed. The next morning, (we don't know why they didn't bother to wash things up the night before) gold was found in the bottom of the cookpot.

Within two years over 5,000 miners had found their way to what had become Tincup Diggings, a tincup full of gold being an average day's yield. Legend has it that Downie offered the town a pan full of gold if the name would be changed to Downieville. Considering the amount of gold laying around, its difficult to imagine that the residents of the town would be overwhelmed by one more pan full, but the name was changed to Downieville.

Downieville also holds the unfortunate distinction of being the only Gold Country town to hang a woman.

Juanita, a dance hall girl, stabbed Jack Cannon, a miner, in the heart with a knife. Although Juanita claimed that Cannon was killed in self defense and that she was pregnant, a lynch mob convicted her and strung her up on the spot. Juanita is said to have slapped the dust off her skirt, shouted, "adios Señors" and leaped off the scaffolding into history.

Busch & Heringlake Country Inn

800/392-7397 916/862-1501
PO Box 68, Sierra City, CA 96125
On the new Yuba Donner Scenic Byway Highway 49

The Busch & Heringlake Country Inn is in the town of Sierra City which sits at the base of the Sierra Buttes mountain that towers 4,000 feet above. The Inn was built in 1871 by A. C. Busch, entrepreneur extraordinaire, and was home to the Wells Fargo Express & Co., Western Union, and an old fashioned general store. The original style has been restored and bits of history furnish the interior.

Handmade windows, wide plank floors, and varnished pine and cedar throughout produce a country elegance that is warm and inviting. Beyond authentic country charm, each room has modern luxury private baths. French windows give

full view of a community overwhelmed by mountain and forest.

Stroll the peaceful streets of Sierra City or take a short ride to the beautiful Lakes Basin recreation area where more that a dozen crystal clear mountain lakes are only minutes apart.

Enjoy hiking, fishing, swimming, bicycling, or just relax next to the scenic Yuba River, a short walk from the Inn. Golfing, horseback riding, or sightseeing throughout the historic Kentucky Mine are only minutes away.

In the evening relax in the warm comfort of our parlor after you enjoy the fine dining available in our Italian Restaurant.

Tortellini al Victorio

4 T. olive oil
2 T. butter
1 cup balsamic vinegar
1 whole red bell pepper

1 whole yellow bell pepper
6 medium size mushrooms
6-8 cloves fresh garlic

Preparation: Cut both types of peppers in half; clean out the seeds; julienne the peppers and the mushrooms to desired size and set aside. After peeling garlic, thinly slice or crush the cloves (your preference). In a large sauté pan, heat the olive oil and add the peppers and mushrooms. When the peppers start to brown, add the garlic. Let these ingredients simmer for about 20 seconds then add the butter and vinegar. After the butter melts, let the sauce reduce slightly. Cook your favorite cheese tortellini; toss with sauce and enjoy! Serves 4 to 5.

Sierra Berry Freeze

1 cup water
½ cup frozen apple juice concentrate
4 cups raspberries or boysenberries
2 T. lemon juice

In a small saucepan combine the water and apple juice concentrate. Bring to a boil; stir and remove from heat. Blend berries in a blender or food processor until smooth. Add lemon juice and water/apple juice mixture. Blend 2-3 seconds. Pour into a bowl; cover and freeze until slushy. Beat with electric mixer until smooth again. Return to bowl and freeze until firm. When ready to serve, let stand at room temperature for 5-10 minutes.

High Country Black Beans & Foothill Nectarines

2½ cups black beans
7½ cups water
2 onions, chopped
5 medium nectarines, peeled and chopped
one 15oz. can tomato sauce
2 cloves garlic, crushed
1/8 cup honey
1 T. chili powder
1 tsp. dry mustard
¼ cup uncooked brown rice

Place beans and water in a large pot. Bring to a boil and boil for 1-2 minutes; remove from heat and let sit for 1 hour. Add onions, bring to a boil again then simmer for 2 hours. Add remaining ingredients and cook 45-60 minutes over low heat.

Serve in large bowls topped with chopped green onions.

Nevada County Gold Country

Photo from color print by Dick James

Nevada County Gold Country

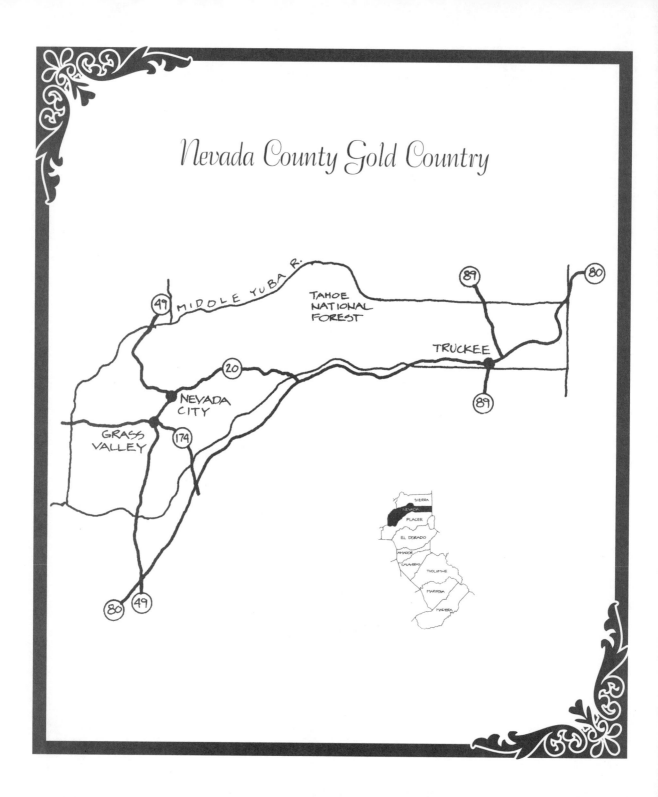

Nevada County

Grass Valley

In 1850, George McKnight was chasing a cow and stubbed his toe on a granite outcropping. His eyes caught a glimmer of gold and this valley was changed forever. Unlike many other Gold Country mining operations, the one in Grass Valley was big business, and used the most sophisticated techniques. The Empire Mine alone yielded more than 5.8 million ounces of gold before it closed in 1956. This one mine produced more gold than the entire Yukon Gold Rush.

George McKnight, an Irishman, may have found the gold but 'Cousin Jack' pulled it out of the rich granite veins. Cornish miners, veterans of the copper and tin mines in their native Cornwall England, were brought in by the mine bosses. The miners were always eager to put in a good word for their relations who more often than not seemed to be their 'Cousin Jack'.

The Cornish feeling still clings to Grass Valley with its 'Cornish Christmas' celebration and the local specialty, pasties. A pastie is a pocket size pie, filled with meat, potatoes, and other savory delights. They are available at any number of places in town, some better than others. Recipes can be found in this book.

1855 brought a devastating fire to Grass Valley which destroyed over 300 structures. The buildings erected after the fire were narrow stone and brick buildings, protected by iron doors and shutters. This type of architecture, which typifies the Gold Country, got its start here in Grass Valley.

A Victorian replica at the corner of Mill and Walsh is the home of Lola Montez. Lola, a.k.a Eliza Gilbert of Ireland, was a dark-haired beauty of Irish and Spanish extraction. She was married and divorced at least three times and was purportedly the mistress of Alexander Dumas, Nicholas I of Russia, Franz Lizst, and King Ludwig of Bavaria. Apparently she didn't invest a great deal of time in any of these relationships because she also had a career as an exotic dancer and an actress.

Her American career began in 1852 with a stop-over in San Francisco. Even then a sophisticated city, patrons were not impressed with her famous spider dance. Apparently this bit of terpsichorean splendor involved wriggling and writhing in a scanty costume. Since San Francisco didn't appreciate her many charms she fled for the gold fields and less urbane tastes. Sadly, even the entertainment starved miners were unimpressed with Lola and she retired to a small house in Grass Valley.

She lived with her current husband and an assortment of animals, including a monkey and a bear. During this period, Lola found herself cast in the role of mentor to young Lotta Crabtree, a child in the neighborhood. Unlike her mentor, Lotta Crabtree became one of the most famous entertainers of her time. She retired early, a wealthy and, by all reports, happy woman.

In contrast, poor Lola tired of Grass Valley and went on tour to Australia in 1855. But she was not successful there nor on a subsequent lecture tour in the United States. Her health, looks and wealthy patrons gone, she died in 1861 at the age of 43.

The Empire Mine State Historic Park and the North Star Mining Museum are important stops when you are in Grass Valley. The Empire Mine is a chance to see a small part of the 360 miles of underground passages hidden beneath the town. The North Star Mining Museum has the world's largest Pelton Wheel, used to run the air compressors that powered the mine.

Nevada City

Nevada City was built on hills with names like Buckeye, Lost, Nabob, Aristocracy, and Prospect. Founded in 1848 and ravaged several times by fire, it survives as one of the most beautiful towns in California. Be sure to pick up a walking tour brochure from the Visitors Center so you don't miss any of the treasures this wonderful town has to offer.

Most miners left the diggings no better off than when they started but Nevada City had some notable exceptions. Herbert Hoover arrived in Nevada City with an engineering degree from Stanford University. He of course went on to the presidency of the United States. It was here that George Hearst acquired the fortune which eventually funded the publishing empire. Benjamin Avery, one of the earliest miners, was a U.S. Minister to China.

One of the most famous names to come out of Nevada City was Madame Eleanor Dumont. Arriving in 1854, proper and well-bred, she opened a gambling parlor, a most unseemly position for a woman. Madame Dumont was also known as Madame Moustache. She followed the gold from camp to camp, carrying her cards and her moustache with her. Sadly, she died by her own hand near Bodie.

Outside of Nevada City, Malakoff Diggins State Historic Park encompasses the old mining town of North Bloomfield. This was the site of a hydraulic mining operation that raised havoc with the rivers and bays downstream. Water blasted away at the hillsides at the rate of almost a million gallons of water per hour.

Today, the devastation wrought by the brutal mining techniques has softened into forms of beauty, reminiscent of Utah's canyonlands.

Pasties—a Grass Valley Tradition

The men of Cornwall, who came to the gold fields looking for their fortune, brought some new mining techniques and a little meat pie that has become a regional favorite. Pastie recipes are a specialty of the Grass Valley area and come in many different varieties. We tried to get a restaurant in the area to part with a recipe to give to you, but it was not to be accomplished. Many bakers are mighty touchy about their "secrets". One lovely lady said she would be happy to share her recipe but could only give us one for 300 pasties.

Here are some from our own kitchens that we thought you would enjoy. But be creative. Let your imagination go, and come up with your own secret recipe.

Pastie Pastry

2 cups all purpose flour 1/3 cup butter
½ tsp. salt 1/3 cup shortening

Mix in a bowl or food processor until the size of small peas. Add ½ cup cold water and mix until the dough just clings; chill in covered bowl for 1 hour.

Divide the pastry into 12 equal parts. Roll into 7 inch rounds and place filling on one side of pastry. Brush edge with water and fold the unfilled side over the filling. Crimp the edge and cut 3 small slits in the top. Place pasties one inch apart on baking sheet and brush with an egg wash of one egg combined with a tablespoon of water.

Bake at 400° for 25-35 minutes. Cool on rack for 15 minutes and serve hot or cold.

Filling Ideas

Beefy Potato

1½ pounds boneless chuck, chopped into ½ inch cubes. Brown in 2 tablespoons oil and remove from pan. Sauté 1 large chopped onion, ½ pound chopped mushrooms, and two cups diced potatoes until nicely browned.

Combine vegetables and beef with 2 cups beef broth. Simmer for one hour; add salt and pepper to taste. Add 1½ tablespoons of cornstarch combined with ½ cup red Sierra Foothill wine and stir until boiling.

Chicken Marsala

Bone five large chicken breasts and cut into ½ inch cubes. Sauté in 3 tablespoons oil with 1 large chopped onion, 1 cup chopped carrots, and 1 cup chopped celery. Cover with chicken broth and simmer for ½ hour. Salt and pepper to taste. Combine ½ cup Marsala with 2 tablespoons cornstarch; add and stir until boiling.

Vegetable

Sauté in ¼ cup water with ½ teaspoon soy sauce, 1 large onion, ½ pound chopped mushrooms, ½ cup chopped celery, 2½ cups chopped bok choy, and 1 cup each chopped carrots and rutabagas, peeled and chopped. Cook for 20 minutes.

Add 1½ cups cubed potatoes and 1½ cups vegetable broth. Simmer 15 minutes and add ½ cup Sierra Foothill white wine with 2 tablespoons cornstarch. Stir until boiling.

Downey House Bed & Breakfast

517 West Broad Street Nevada City, CA 95959
800/258-2815 916/265-2815

Discover Nevada City hospitality and charm at the historic Downey House, a romantic bed & breakfast inn overlooking town from the top of Broad Street.

Built in 1869, and occupied for many years by the Downey family, this Eastlake-style Victorian home has been thoughtfully restored to its century-old airy elegance.

Downey House is clustered amid Nevada City's noted Victorians atop Nabob Hill and is just a block from the downtown historic district.

From the welcoming gate, curved veranda, and lush landscaping that adorn its exterior, to the winding hallways, bright, clean rooms, and upstairs sun porch with treetop views, Downey House captures the flavor of days gone by. The entrance room from our garden has homemade brownies, coffee, and tea for our guests.

Each of the six comfortable, soundproofed rooms has its own private bath with tub and shower, and a queen or double bed with down comforters. The downstairs parlor provides a common meeting place.

In the morning, the aroma of fresh ground coffee drifts through the halls of Downey House. On cool days, the generous breakfast buffet may be enjoyed in the kitchen, parlor or sun room. When it is warm, guests may choose the garden, terrace, or veranda.

The relaxing garden area has a lily pond in the shadows of a restored red barn from the 1800s and plenty of room for sunning and casual conversation. Wine is served in the parlor every evening at 5:00 and fresh fruit is always available.

Downey House Apple Bread

Mix together 1½ cups sugar, 1/3 cup salad oil and 2 eggs. Add:

1½ cup flour	1 tsp. nutmeg
2 tsp. cinnamon	½ tsp. allspice
2 tsp. baking soda	1 tsp. salt

Mix well and add:
2 peeled medium size green apples, diced
½ cup chopped nuts   ½ cup raisins or chopped dates

Mix well; dough will be stiff. (Use your hands.) Bake in a 5 x 9 loaf pan in a 350° oven for 1 hour and 15 minutes.

Placer County Gold Country

Photo from color print by Dick James

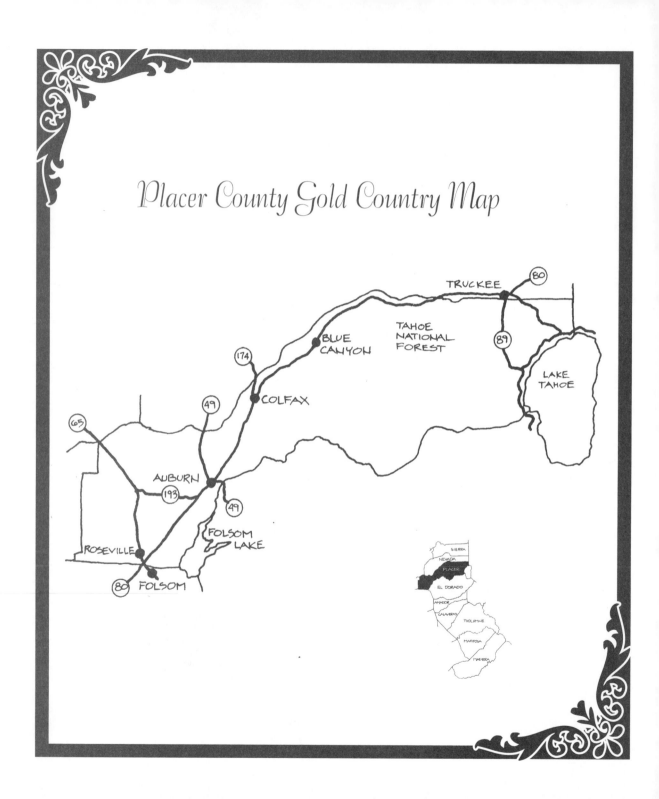

Placer County Gold Country Map

Placer County Gold Country

Visitor Information 800/427-6463 or 916/887-2111

Auburn

Auburn was one of the earliest mining camps. In 1848, a party of miners organized by Claude Chana, three other Frenchmen, and a small group of Indians began panning by a stream now known as Auburn Ravine. The first three pans turned up sizable nuggets and the seed that would grow to become Auburn was sprouted.

Originally known as North Fork Dry Diggins, Auburn turned out to be a rich site indeed. It was not uncommon for a miner to wash out $1,000 to $1,500 in a single day. By 1850, over 1,500 miners were working the Auburn Ravine. Among this group were members of the Volunteer Regiment out of Auburn New York who renamed the area.

Geography, not gold, kept Auburn alive. Situated at the confluence of the middle and north forks of the American River, Auburn became a trading center. In the early 1860s, it was determined that the transcontinental railroad would pass through Auburn, sparing it the fate of so many gold towns.

Today Auburn is the biggest and busiest of the Gold Country towns. Interstate 80 runs through town as does Highway 49. The railroad is still moving along the same route it has taken for over a century. Although currently a suburb of Sacramento, Auburn has not forgotten its golden past.

Old Town Auburn has become something of a mecca for antique shops which are mostly housed in historic buildings. Visit the Placer County Courthouse and Museum and the Gold Country Museum which features artifacts from the Maidu Indians and from the Chinese settlers.

Coloma

The first of many boom towns, Coloma became home to 10,000 hopeful souls during the Gold Rush. In the early days of gold fever, goods were sparse and prices were astronomical. This characteristic was true at every mining camp. In fact, it was probably more profitable to be a shopkeeper than a miner. Sam Brannon, the man who carried the tale of gold to San Francisco, thought so. History has it that he made a tidy (no pun intended) fortune by selling $50 shovels to the argonauts.

A reproduction of Sutter's Mill was dedicated 120 years to the day after Marshall's fateful discovery. The Marshall Gold Discovery State Historic Park Museum is across the highway from Sutter's Mill and offers the visitor much information about the history of the area's past.

Sacramento County Gold Country

Photo from color print by Dick James

Sacramento County Gold Country

Visitor Information 916/264-7777

In 1839 the Mexican governor of California granted 47,800 acres of land to John Sutter, a native of Switzerland who had deserted his wife and children when he fled his native land to escape debtors prison.

Sutter began to build his adobe fort at the confluence of the Sacramento and American Rivers, laying the groundwork for what would become Sacramento, the state capital of California.

Sutter eventually lost everything to a combination of bad luck and bad debt but the settlement thrived, fed by its proximity to the gold fields.

Because Sacramento is a large, modern city you have to do a bit of digging for the historic, but it is here. You just need to know where to look. Sutter's Fort Historic Park is a faithful reproduction of the original and the State Indian Museum will give you an excellent overview of the first residents of the state.

Old Sacramento has been transformed from a rundown river front to a charming area with wooden sidewalks and a terrific collection of restored buildings, filled with museums, shops, and restaurants.

Hartley House Bed & Breakfast Inn

700 22nd Street Sacramento, CA 95816
Corner of 22nd & G Streets in Midtown
916/447-7829 800/831-5806 Fax 916/447-1820

Stunning turn-of-the-century mansion located in historic Boulevard Park, in Midtown Sacramento. This fully restored Colonial Revival features original hardwood floors, stained glass windows, and a 12 foot long bay window seat in the fully appointed parlor.

Catering to both the business and vacationing traveler, the inn's five rooms each have a distinctive personality; all have private baths, queen or double bed, robes, TV, clocks, and telephones. A full breakfast featuring house blend coffee and juices, as well as fresh seasonal fruit, is served each morning in the dining room. And the cookie jar in the dining room is always stocked with freshly baked cookies.

Within 20 blocks of the inn are the Capitol, Old Town, Convention Center, downtown business district, shopping, and the finest restaurants and coffee and dessert houses in Sacramento.

Games, maps, menus, and Sacramento history books are available. For summer visitors, Hartley House is fully air-conditioned.

Stuffed French Toast with Strawberry Sauce

4 eggs
1 cup lowfat milk
1 tsp. cinnamon (in the winter) or 1/8 cup orange juice (in the summer)
4 slices sourdough bread (use oversized loaves with slices approx 3" x 5")
4 oz. softened light cream cheese
2 cups whole frozen strawberries, no sugar added

Place strawberries in microwave-safe bowl. Microwave on high 4 minutes, then check. Repeat until strawberries are juicy. Place in serving bowl.

Beat eggs and milk, mix in cinnamon or orange juice, set aside. Spread cream cheese on one side each slice of bread, then put two slices together to form a sandwich. Slice each sandwich in half. Dip in egg mixture. Cook on a buttered griddle until brown on both sides.

Serve French toast with strawberry sauce on the side. Makes 4 servings.

Amber House

1313 22nd Street Sacramento, CA 95816
Eight blocks east of State Capitol; between Capitol Street & N Street
916/444-8085 800/755-6526 Fax 916/447-1548

The Amber House offers deluxe accommodations in two meticulously restored vintage structures.

The Poet's Refuge, a 1905 Craftsman style home touched with period elegance offers five guest rooms, all with private baths, one with a Jacuzzi tub for two.

The Artist's Retreat is a fully restored 1913 Mediterranean style home, which offers four luxurious guest rooms with marble tiled baths and large Jacuzzi bathtubs for two. The Van Gogh room in this home features a spectacular solarium bathroom with a heart shaped Jacuzzi tub and waterfall.

All rooms have cable TV, private telephones (modem ready) and central air conditioning. A full gourmet breakfast is served in the guest room, the dining room or on the patio outside, and bikes are available, including a tandem.

Whatever your mood, you'll find the warm hospitality and personal attention you deserve. The inn is located in a residential neighborhood of historic homes just eight blocks east of the State Capitol near other historic sights, shops, and restaurants.

Swiss Mustard Eggs

(makes single serving)

1 English muffin, toasted	1 T. stone ground mustard
3 eggs	1 T. grated Parmesan
¼ cup grated Swiss cheese	2 strips bacon
2 T. milk	1/8 tsp. pepper

Mix eggs with milk, mustard, and pepper, using wire whisk. Cook bacon till crisp; crumble and set aside. Melt ½ tablespoon butter in skillet. Add egg mixture and scramble. When almost done, add Swiss cheese and bacon. Cook till cheese melts.

Place muffin on plate, spoon eggs onto both halves; sprinkle with the Parmesan. Garnish plate with quartered tomato slices and sprouts.

23

History of Gold Prospecting Processes

In spite of the rumors that drifted out of the gold fields, most of the time gold was not laying around waiting to be scooped up. Mother Nature didn't give her booty up without a struggle and the miners had a number of methods to extract the precious metal.

Panning is the simplest way to separate gold from rocks and dirt. Very simply, shovel gravel and dirt into a shallow pan, add water and swish this around. The water and gravel should slosh over the sides, leaving the heavier gold at the bottom of the pan. Don't let it spill out or you'll be very annoyed with yourself. This method is effective but not terribly efficient. A miner would probably be limited to fifty or sixty pans a day. Miners quickly began devising more efficient ways of making their dreams come true.

The next step up in technology was the rocker. The rocker was a large rectangular box, set on an angle where dirt and water were poured over cleats. A screen at the top of the rocker caught the biggest rocks. This was a popular method at the dry diggings, since the water could be added in bucketfuls. The rocker made mining much more efficient for catching the coarsegold and mercury was added to the rockers to trap the finer gold "flour".

The sluice box was the rocker on a larger scale. Sometimes several boxes would be hooked together with a team of miners working the line.

Horribly destructive, yet very efficient, hydraulic mining was introduced in 1853. Imagine a high pressure fire hose turned on a snowbank, quickly dissolving the snow. That was the effect on the hillsides of the Gold Country. Whole mountainsides of dirt and gravel were washed into the sluice and then into the rivers, lakes, and ultimately into the San Francisco Bay. By the mid 1880s this type of mining had been stopped. Ironically, although it was efficient at getting the gold out of the mountains, much of the gold was lost to the fast-moving water. Secondary mining operations were set up downstream of the sluices and were often quite successful.

Quartz mining sent the miners underground to bring out the gold-bearing ore. Once the ore was above ground it was crushed or stamped into a dust. Originally, panning was used to separate the gold from the ore but once again this was found to be too inefficient. Through the use of mercury and cyanide the miners were able to recover over 90 percent of the gold.

A variation on this method is in use today at large scale mining facilities throughout the world.

Many museums in California's Gold Country offer exhibits of the equipment that was actually in use during the gold rush and up into the more contemporary times.

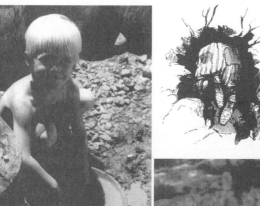

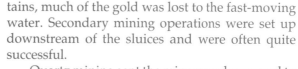

El Dorado Gold Country

Photo from color print by Dick James

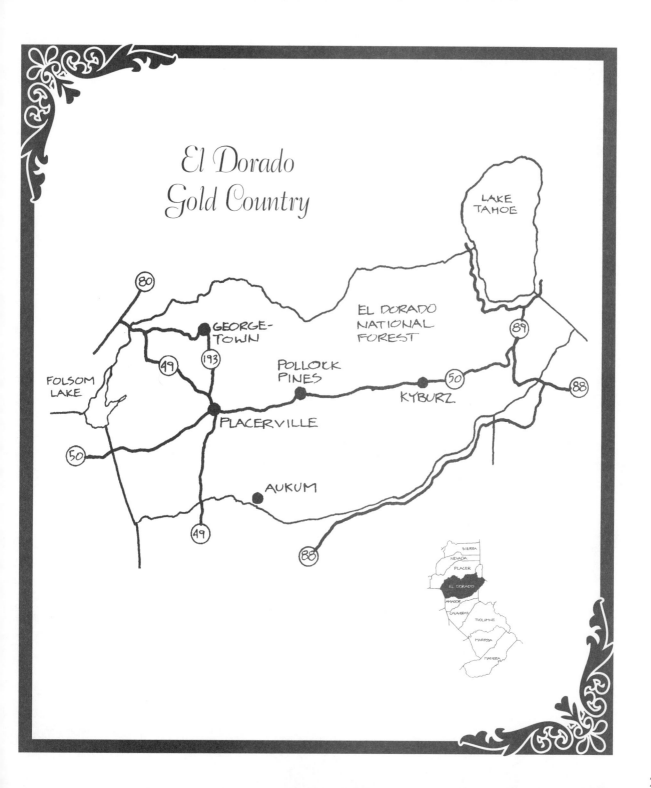

El Dorado
Gold Country

LAKE TAHOE

EL DORADO NATIONAL FOREST

FOLSOM LAKE

GEORGE-TOWN

POLLOCK PINES

KYBURZ

PLACERVILLE

AUKUM

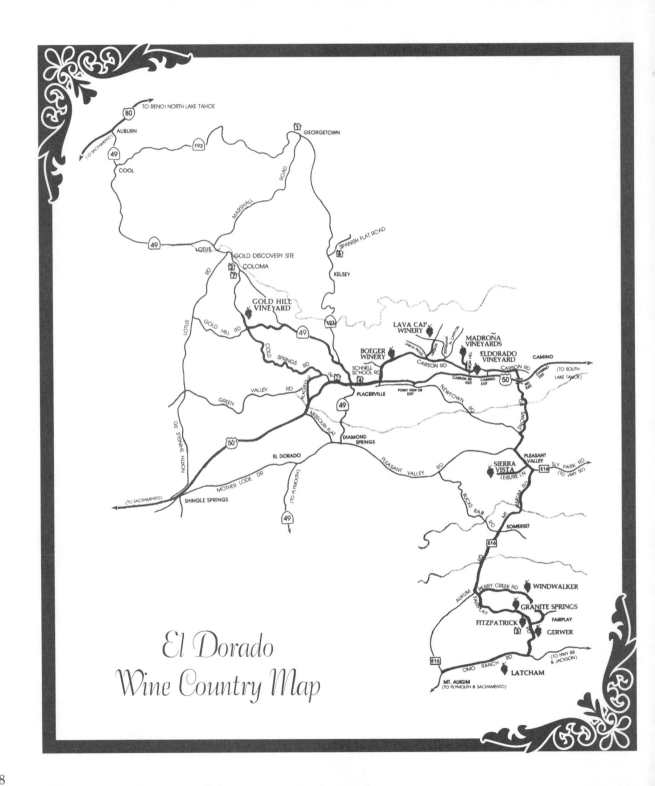

El Dorado
Wine Country Map

El Dorado Gold Country

Visitor Information 800/457-6279 916/621-5885

Placerville

Claims in this area were yielding five pounds of gold per week and the people flowed into a spot known as Dry Diggins. Easy money and a transient population don't bring out the best in town life and pretty soon they were stringing the varmints up by the necks, hence the name Hangtown.

In 1854, Hangtown's name was changed to Placerville. Big mistake. If the poet in your soul wants to call it Hangtown, do so proudly.

Hangtown was typically a wild and woolly place, but it was also home, if even for a brief time, to Mark Hopkins who, at that time ran the grocery store. Mr. Hopkins later ran the Central Pacific Railroad.

Twenty year old Philip Armour walked from his family's New York farm to California in 1849. Five years later he opened up a butcher shop in Hangtown, launching what would become one of the largest meat processing companies in the country.

A wagon maker named John Studebaker, spent five years in Hangtown making wheelbarrows and saving enough money to start an automobile factory in his native Indiana.

History also reminds us of Miss 'Immigrant Jane' Stuart who drove a herd of horses across the plains and over the mountains to Hangtown. She sold the horses and bought a house on Main Street which she turned into a house of ill-repute. (Frankly it probably had a pretty good reputation with the local miners.)

Some of old Hangtown can be found in Placerville today. City Hall sits next to the house that Immigrant Jane built for her ladies. Many of the older buildings have been given facades through the years so don't be afraid to walk around the back to get a real feel for the place.

The Gold Bug Mine, owned by the town, has daily tours of the mine shaft and stamp mill. This is one of the places where you can see the quartz vein and get a sense about hardrock mining.

Hangtown
Fry

There are a number of theories about the origin of California's most famous egg dish, Hangtown Fry. Some say it was a local miner showing off by ordering the three rarest items on the menu; eggs, oysters, and bacon. Another theory holds that those three items weren't rare at all and were, in fact, the only ingredients that local cooks had at their disposal. These are both possible but they lack romance and whimsy.

My favorite story is that Hangtown Fry was created the night before a hanging. The condemned man, in an effort to buy time so that his pals could spring him, requested a meal made with eggs, bacon, and that great rarity Olympia oysters. Since tradition holds that a last meal can't be denied, the search for the small oysters began. It took several days for the oysters to be located and in that time his comrades were able to break him out of jail.

½ pound bacon
1 pint small oysters
corn meal
6 eggs
¼ cup chopped parsley
Preheat oven to 350°. Chop bacon and fry until crisp in heavy iron skillet. Remove bacon and drain off most of the grease. Dredge the oysters in corn meal and fry in grease until they begin to curl. Beat eggs with parsley and a little water. Pour mixture over bacon and oysters which have been returned to the pan. Place in oven for 10 minutes.

Serve with champagne and biscuits. But stay away from ropes and trees.

Boeger Winery

1709 Carson Road Placerville, CA 95667
Hangtown area: from Highway 50, North on Schnell School Road,
right 1/3 mile · 916/622-8094 Fax 916/622-8112

The family owned and operated winery was established in 1972 on the site of one of California's oldest wineries. Boeger was the first modern day winery to locate in El Dorado, a region that compares with the best winegrape growing areas throughout the world.

Owner-winemaker Greg Boeger, whose wines have won numerous awards in competitions and have received national attention and recognition, follows in the family tradition of 100 years of personal dedication to the production of premium wines. His grandfather, Anton Nichelini, started a winery in Napa County in 1890 that is still family owned and operated.

The Boeger Tasting Room is housed in their historic stone cellar built in 1872 and listed on the National Registry of Historic Places. Visitors are welcome every day from 10am to 5pm all year except traditional family holidays. Picnicking under the ancient fig trees is encouraged. Larger groups and families are easily accommodated in the spacious picnic grounds.

Historic Cellar at Boeger Winery

BBQ'd Butterflied Leg of Lamb

Cultivate a good butcher and have him bone, trim, and butterfly a leg of lamb, neatly. You need ½ pound of meat per person.
Make a thick marinade with:

½ cup Grey Poupon mustard	½-¾ cup fresh rosemary, chopped
¼ cup soy sauce	2 T. fresh, coarse ground pepper
2 T. olive oil	1 tsp. salt

Make a thick paste and rub it all around the nooks and crannies of the meat and let it sit at room temperature for at least 4 hours.

It is best grilled over mesquite, but any barbecue will do, for about 20 minutes on a side. Use a meat thermometer and cook rare.

Lava Cap Winery

916/621-0175 800/475-0175 Fax 916/621-4399
2221 Fruitridge Road Placerville, CA 95667

Located in the Apple Hill region, Lava Cap Winery is a small family owned and operated winery dedicated to the production of premium, estate bottled wines. During the harvest the grapes are handpicked and brought directly to the winery for immediate crushing. Our winemaker, Thomas Jones, hand crafts our wines using the latest technology, coupled with his skills acquired at UC Davis, where he earned a graduate degree in oenology.

All six members of the Jones family work to produce our premium wines for your enjoyment.

Taste the wines in our lovely redwood tasting room. Bring a picnic to enjoy on our sundeck and linger over a bottle of Lava Cap wine with the fresh mountain air and scenic view. For cozy tasting during winter, the tasting room is complete with a wood stove. We are open daily from 11:00am to 5:00pm, except major family holidays.

Tours and groups are welcome on our spacious grounds. Please call the winery to arrange for your arrival time and special tour. We will gladly ship wine directly to your family and friends throughout the year.

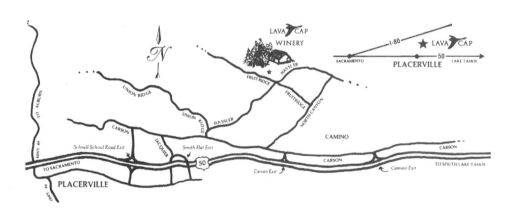

Lava Cap Fruit Cocktail

Prepare fresh strawberries and pineapple chunks in individual serving dishes. Sprinkle lightly with sugar and marinate in Lava Cap Muscat. Serve with shortbread or over vanilla ice cream.

American River Inn

PO Box 43 Georgetown, CA 95634
Main Street at Orleans Street Georgetown
916/333-4499 800/245-6566

Innkeepers Will and Maria Collin carry on the century old tradition of graciousness in a setting far removed from the fast pace of modern living. True luxury in a country setting greets guests who are made to feel at home. The American River Inn with its 18 elegant rooms and lovely country suites recreates a time of nostalgia and relaxation for its patrons.

The Queen Anne House is one of three honeymoon suites. Comprising half the second floor, it includes a king sized bed, balcony patio and fireplace. French doors open to a private bath that features a dual spa tub as well as separate shower.

The other honeymoon retreats are in the newly renovated third floor of the main building. These rooms, dominated by fluffy queen sized beds, each feature a fireplace.

As visitors, you awaken to the delight of a lovely breakfast served by your innkeepers in the dining room or on the patio. You may wish to stroll through Victorian gardens, enjoy the dove aviary, or take a hot jacuzzi at the refreshing mountain stream pool.

Spend your afternoons on the inn's putting green, mini-driving range, or badminton court. Or borrow a bicycle for exploring. We will even make arrangements for river rafting trips while you are in the area.

Lemon Date Pecan Muffins

½ cup brown sugar
6 T. unsalted butter
5 T. lemon juice
½ tsp. baking soda
¼ cup honey
½ cup sour cream
1 egg

1¾ cup flour
1½ tsp. baking powder
¾ tsp. salt
1 cup chopped dates
1 cup chopped pecans
¼ cup hot water
1 T. grated lemon peel

Preheat oven to 400°

Cook brown sugar, butter, lemon juice, and honey in saucepan until hot. Whisk sour cream, egg, and lemon peel in bowl. Whisk in brown sugar mixture.

Combine flour, baking powder, baking soda, and salt in another bowl. Add to liquid ingredients and stir. Add dates and pecans and hot water; stir until blended.

Bake 20 minutes in 14 buttered muffin cups.

Latcham Vineyards

209/245-6834, 3913, 6642 · 800/750-5578
PO Box 80 Mt. Aukum, CA 95656 · 2860 Omo Ranch Road Mt. Aukum
One mile east of Mt. Aukum & Highway E16

Latcham Vineyards, family owned and operated, was established in 1981. It is located on the north slope of Mt. Aukum Valley, a site chosen for its beauty, fine soil, and excellent growing conditions.

Among the wide variety of fine wines featured here are Zinfandel, Cabernet Sauvignon, Petite Sirah, Cabernet Franc, Chardonnay, Sauvignon Blanc, White Zinfandel, Port, and Red and White table wines.

The tasting room is open Wednesday through Sunday 11am to 5pm, and by appointment. Mail orders are welcome. The public is invited to taste and discuss wines, tour the vineyards and picnic under the oak trees.

Orange Nut Bread

Mix grated rind from 4 oranges with ¾ cup water and 1 cup sugar. Cook until consistency of applesauce. Set aside.

Mix 1 cup sugar, 2 eggs well beaten, 1 cup milk, 3¼ cups flour, 3 teaspoons baking powder, 2 tablespoons butter, ½ teaspoon salt, and 1 cup chopped nutmeats.

When thoroughly mixed, combine with peel mixture. Mix well but do not beat. Pour into 2 well buttered loaf pans and bake at 325° for 35 to 40 minutes.

Fitzpatrick Winery & Lodge

7740 Fairplay Road Somerset, CA 95684
18 miles southeast of Placerville; 17 miles east of Plymouth
209/245-3248 Fax 209/245-6838

Atop a hill commanding a view of El Dorado's wine country and beyond in all directions, our hand-built, massive log lodge is home to Fitzpatrick Winery & Lodge and the Fitzpatrick family. Situated on 40 acres, the Lodge offers four rooms for bed and breakfast accommodations, each with private baths and balconies.

The rooms have their own personalities aptly named 'The Log Suite', 'The Irish Room', 'The French-Basque Room' and 'The Olde Fairplay Room'.

The foothill country setting and expansive view guarantees deep relaxation and a respite from everyday life. Winetasting and tea every night and breakfast comes with many made to order choices.

A couple of times each month Fitzpatrick's is alive with our famous ethnic theme dinners from around the world. Request our biannual newsletter and calendar of events.

A thousand welcomes!!!!

Eggs Toby

Two eggs sunnyside up steamed in Marsala with melted sharp white cheddar cheese and smoked salmon layered on an 'Irish' muffin.

Madroña Vineyards

PO Box 454 Camino, CA 95709 · High Hill Road Camino
From Highway 50 take Carson Road exit 5 miles east of Placerville. Go west on
Carson Road ¼ mile and turn right on High Hill Road · 916/644-5948

In 1973, Dick and Leslie Bush planted 35 acres of vines on a scenic ridge located at the 3,000 foot elevation; the highest vineyard in California. The warm days and cool nights of this distinct microclimate have proven to produce a fruit with excellent sugar-acid balance and varietal character.

Using hand picked grapes selected for their optimum flavor, ripeness, and acidity, the family started making their own wines in 1980. The combination of climate, traditional winemaking techniques and caring supervision have produced wines that consistently receive gold and silver awards.

We invite you to try a variety of wines in our tasting room. Special release wines are available at the winery. We are very proud of these unique wines and feel no tasting would be complete without them.

The wooded area which surrounds the winery provides a scenic foothill setting for picnics and the owners and winemaker are generally available for tours. We are open daily from 11:00am to 5:00pm.

Madroña Raviolis

This traditional Italian recipe is made in three steps. The longer the sauce simmers, the better it is.

Tomato Sauce

2 T. olive oil
1 onion, chopped fine
2 cloves garlic, minced
Four 15oz. cans tomato sauce

Two 6oz. cans tomato paste
3 cups water
1 cup minced parsley
Two 3½ oz. cans mushrooms and juice

salt, pepper, rosemary, marjoram and thyme to taste
In a large saucepan heat oil; add onion and garlic. Cook until lightly browned. Add rest of ingredients and cook slowly for 4 hours or longer.

Filling

½ onion, minced very fine
1½ cloves garlic, minced very fine
¼ cup parsley, chopped fine

½ cup grated Parmesan cheese
2 or 3 eggs
pinch each of thyme and marjoram

2 lbs. Italian sausage with casing removed
two 10oz. pkgs. frozen spinach, cooked, drained and chopped fine
Mix all ingredients except eggs; add eggs and mix. It should be a good spreading consistency. Add a speck of thyme and marjoram. Refrigerate until ready to use.

Pasta

4 cups flour
2 eggs

½ tsp. salt
lukewarm water

Mix flour, eggs, and salt. Add enough lukewarm water to make a firm but elastic dough. Knead on floured board for 5 minutes. Let dough rest 10 minutes. Break dough into 2 or 3 rounds. Roll each round very thin. Spread some filling over half of each round. Fold the other half over the filling. Roll with ravioli rolling pin and cut apart, Put on floured pan in a single layer, sift a little flour on top and let dry for 1 hour. Cook in boiling salted water for 20 minutes and serve with hot tomato sauce.

Historic Emigrant Trail

California's Gold Rush of 1848 inspired the most crazed, adventurous and courageous migration in United States history. Across the plains and through deserts on the Overland Trail, pioneers traveled more than 2,000 miles to face the rugged Sierra as the last barrier to the wealth of the Sacramento Valley. Today, remnants and scars of this migration may still be seen in Hope Valley, a territory known for both its natural beauty and historic character.

Sorensen's Resort (see next page) has created a leisurely hiking tour which will lead participants across parts of the Mormon-Emigrant trail and the early Pony Express route; where you can touch grooved and rust stained rocks; photograph signature rocks dated 1849; see Snowshoe Thompson's historic cave and hear his story; find out about the earliest Pony Express route and why it was only used for a few months.

Sorensen's Resort

14255 Highway 88 Hope Valley, CA 96120
916/694-2203 800/423-9949

Sorensen's Resort in Hope Valley is nestled on 165 acres of aspen and pine forest at 7,000 feet in the rugged Sierra Nevada. This friendly cluster of cabins offers a full range of year round recreational opportunities; cross-country skiing, great fishing, unlimited hiking and leisurely biking or mountain biking.

This historic settlement sponsors Emigrant Trail hiking tours, watercolor seminars, cooking classes, fly-fishing instruction, nature photo workshops, a full service cross-country ski center in the winter and wedding and honeymoon packages. A private creekside gazebo is available for special events.

Accommodations range from inexpensive cozy cabins to the more deluxe chalets. Sorensen's is close to the scenic delights of Lake Tahoe and the relaxing hot spring of Grover State Park. Sorensen's Country Cafe serves breakfast, lunch, and dinner daily, featuring breakfast specials of waffles, quiches,

homemade muffins, and fresh fruit, and their famous trademark soups and stews for lunch and dinner. Dinner meals also feature a wonderful selection of fresh fish dishes, pastas, and grilled entrees.

For a relaxing high Sierra visit where fine wines, select imported beers and wonderful culinary experiences await travelers, Sorensen's is the place to call.

Classic Beef Burgundy Stew

6 lbs. lean stew meat, cut to bite size pieces
6-8 brown potatoes, cubed, peeled or unpeeled

10-12 cloves garlic	1 large onion, cubed
1 cube butter	4 stalks celery, sliced
one 50oz. can beef consomme	10 mushrooms, sliced
1 cup red burgundy wine	3 T. dry parsley
2 T. Knoor beef base	4 T. dry sweet basil
6-8 carrots, sliced	4 bay leaves

ground pepper & garlic salt to taste
¼ cup cornstarch/stir with hot water until a smooth, just slightly thick mixture forms

Brown meat thoroughly, one frying pan full at a time, with butter and garlic, pepper and garlic salt. Put into large stew or soup pot with beef consomme, wine, onion, spices, and beef base. Bring to a boil and simmer for one hour until meat is tender. Add carrots, celery, potatoes, and mushrooms and cook until tender. Adjust seasonings to taste. Thicken with cornstarch mixture. Serves 15-20.

Amador Gold Country

Photo from color print by Dick James

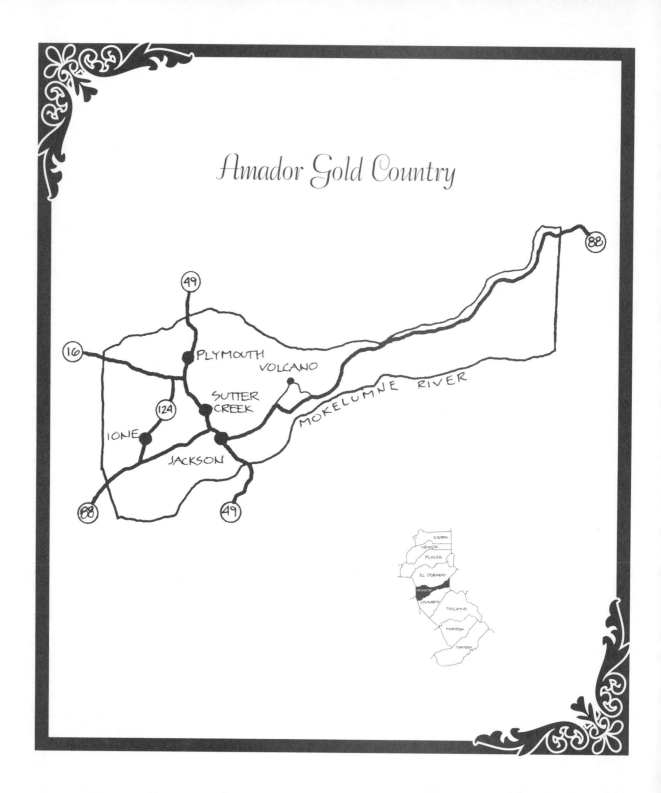

Amador Gold Country

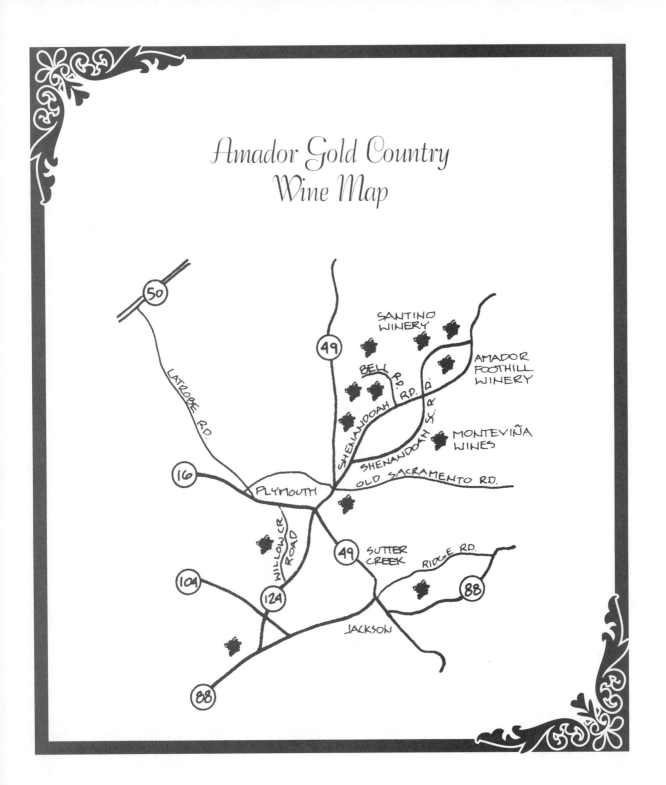

Amador Gold Country
Wine Map

41

Amador Gold Country

Visitor Information 800/649-4988 209/223-0350

Sutter Creek

John Marshall discovered gold in 1848, but what he left behind for posterity is the name Sutter Creek. The town got its start when several miners erected a large tent to use on rainy days off when they could not get as far as the "big" cities of Jackson or Drytown.

Sutter Creek boasts some grand old stories to go along with the historic atmosphere. The owner of the Old Eureka Mine was a woman named Hetty Green. In her day Ms. Green was known as the richest woman in the world. And not because of a lucrative divorce either. Hetty was a Wall Street financial genius.

Leland Stanford, railroad king, U.S. Senator, Governor of California and founder of Stanford University staked his claim in Sutter Creek, too. As he came minutes from signing away his claim which had suffered repeated failures, his foreman talked him out of it and only a short time later a big strike was made.

Still a great place to visit during any kind of weather, Sutter Creek is well known for its quaint charm, well preserved buildings, unique shops and interesting antique hideaways.

Volcano

A short detour along Highway 88 will lead you to the famous Indian Grinding Rock Historic Park. The site contains the largest grinding stones found in America as well as a wonderful reproduction of a Mi-Wuk village. The Mi-Wuks inhabited much of the central area of the Gold Country.

The community of Volcano, once a very sophisticated place for a mining camp, holds title to the first public library, the first observatory and the first debating and literary societies in California. But don't let this facade of intellectuality fool you. It also had three dozen saloons and three breweries.

Volcano has been beautifully and lovingly restored and is well worth the detour.

Just a few miles northeast of Volcano is Daffodil Hill. The owners, the Mclaughlin family, annually open to the public a four acre plot of their ranch which they have kept planted with hundreds of thousands of daffodil bulbs. The display is incredible. Mid to late March is a peak time, but it all depends on Mother Nature.

Jackson

Unlike most of the gold towns, Jackson grew slowly. Hardrock mining made this town and gave it a stability not often found in other parts of the Gold Country.

The Kennedy Mine, founded in 1856, operated until 1942 when the war effort made mercury and explosives difficult to find. You can still visit the huge tailing wheels of the mine in a park just north of town. At one time the Kennedy and Argonaut mines were the deepest in the world.

At one point in its nefarious history, Jackson had a reputation due to the number of brothels that survived the gold rush and lasted into the 1950s. Yes, dears. You heard right. Not so very long ago. In fact, in 1968 a plaque was erected to the soiled doves of Jackson.

Amador Harvest Inn

21455 Steiner Road Plymouth, CA 95669
209/245-5512

The beautiful and verdant Shenandoah Valley in Amador County is home to many fabulous wineries and charming inns. One of the nicest of these is the Amador Harvest Inn. Tucked serenely amidst the beauty of rolling vineyards, elegant oak trees, and shimmering lakes the Amador Harvest Inn proudly boasts of serenity and a peaceful haven.

Enjoy the ultimate in Bed & Breakfast Inns with four elegantly appointed rooms. Privacy is at its best since all rooms offer private baths. Each guest room is light and airy with accents of majestic oak and brass, and all are radiantly decorated in full floral splendor. The views from each room offer tranquil vistas of the Inn's prized lakes and lush vineyards.

Visit our winery and tasting room; stroll the spacious grounds; or relax with a good book in our reading room. To add to the warmth of the delightful Amador Harvest Inn, you are in for a treat from Bobbie's kitchen.

A full country breakfast will be served each morning at 9:00am.

Grand Marnier French Toast

6 eggs beaten
1 cup orange juice
1 loaf sweet French bread, sliced
Powdered sugar
1 cup whipping cream
1 to 1½ oz. Grand Marnier
Butter or cooking oil

Mix eggs, heavy cream and orange juice. Add Grand Marnier to taste. Dip bread into egg mixture and put into large baking dish. Cover with seal wrap and refrigerate over night. Heat griddle to 325°. Brown on each side; when done keep warm in oven. Dust with powdered sugar and serve.

Indian Creek Bed & Breakfast

21950 Highway 49 Plymouth, CA 95669 · 209/245-4648 800/24-CREEK
3 miles north of Plymouth on Historic Highway 49

Serene as a mountain retreat on ten quiet acres, this magnificent 1932 log lodge was a Hollywood producer's wedding gift to his Ziegfield Follies bride.

Indian Creek was opened in 1990 after reviving its meticulously crafted log interior with stunning Douglas fir floors. Dominating the cathedral ceiling living room is a two story fireplace made of selected quartz rocks and a beautiful Chamber piano from 1872. A sunny sitting/reading room is adjacent to the dining room with antique pine furniture.

Up the stairs, overlooking the living room is a log and manzanita balcony that accesses four beautiful guest rooms which are decorated for the ladies that inspired them. Each has a queen size bed, antiques, private bathrooms, and two have balconies and fireplaces.

Spend the afternoon antiquing or winetasting; enjoy appetizers near the pool in summer or in front of a fire in winter; have dinner at a nearby restaurant; soak in the hot tub; and awaken to a full gourmet breakfast.

Lemon Soufflé Pancakes

6 eggs separated	4 tsp. fresh lemon juice
½ tsp. salt	4 T. grated rind
¼ cup vegetable oil	4 tsp. baking powder
2 T. maple syrup	1 cup unbleached flour
2 cups small curd cottage cheese	

Start griddle; beat egg whites until stiff but not dry; combine all other ingredients, blending until smooth. Fold in egg whites; spoon onto griddle baking until bubbling; turn over and cook until bottom is done. Serve with favorite toppings. Serves 4 to 6.

We often serve the muffins with fresh strawberry or melon sorbet and the pancakes with sliced turkey ham.

Chewy Orange Raisin Muffins

2 eggs	1 cup flour
1 cup sugar	1 tsp. baking powder
1 tsp. vanilla	1 cup raisins
½ orange, peel & all, chopped	

Beat together first 3 ingredients; add orange and beat with flour and other ingredients. Divide into 12 paper lined muffin cups and bake at 350° for 20-25 minutes.

Santino Winery

12225 Steiner Road Plymouth, CA 95669
Corner of Steiner & Upton Roads 5 miles east of
Plymouth up Shenandoah Road 209/242-6979

Surrounded by the pastoral beauty of the Gold Country's Shenandoah Valley, Santino Winery stands as a tribute to excellence in winemaking. Since 1979, Santino has been producing noble wines from the soil of Amador Gold Country. From the sparkling freshness of a delicate blush to the bold earthiness of rich reds, the wines of Santino have been recognized as some of the finest in the country.

Since the release of the winery's first Zinfandel over a decade ago, Santino has demonstrated a dedication to producing wines of the best possible quality.

As a reflection of this commitment, winemaker Scott Harvey was recently distinguished as one of the ten best winemakers in the nation. He possesses a boundless enthusiasm for his craft, expressing a spirit and energy for every new production he undertakes.

Harvey's background began in Germany, where he served his winemaking apprenticeship. There he learned to create spectacular late-harvest white wines, to which he has added a matchless mastery of Amador reds. He is a true perfectionist, with a respect for tradition and a vision for invention.

Enjoy tours and tastings at Santino Winery every weekend from 12:00 noon to 4:30pm or by appointment.

Pasta Angelica

1 lb fresh angel hair pasta, cooked al dente
(This recipe is far better using fresh from the garden vegetables and herbs)
5 fresh large tomatoes, chopped
1 small white onion, minced
2 large cloves garlic, crushed
5-6 fresh basil leaves, torn
1 T. olive oil
½ cup Santino Zinfandel
Gently sauté tomatoes, onion, and garlic in olive oil until soft and aromatic. Add basil leaves and wine; simmer for 5 minutes.

Toss with angel hair pasta and sprinkle lightly with fresh grated Parmesan or Asiago cheese.

Serve with dark greens and balsamic vinegar.

Monteviña

PO Box 100 Plymouth, CA 95669
20680 Shenandoah School Road Plymouth
209/245-6942

Monteviña, the largest winery in Amador County, has recently embarked on an exciting new Italian program that features vineyards of Sangiovese, Nebbiolo, Aleatico, Refosco, and some forty other Italian varieties. With climate and soils similar to those of Italian wine regions, Amador and the grapes of Italy are a perfect fit.

Monteviña currently makes an exceptional Reserve Barbera, as well as Zinfandel, Cabernet Sauvignon, Chardonnay, and Fumé Blanc. Make Monteviña a destination during your visit to the Gold Country. Stop by and taste wines that have earned praise from wine writers across the country. Bring your lunch or a snack to enjoy in the lovely shaded picnic area surrounded by the vineyards of Italy...in Amador.

Chicken Satay with Almond Butter Sauce

The smoky, citrus, and herb aromas and rich, spicy, fruity flavors of Monteviña's 1991 Fumé Blanc perfectly complement this dish.

1 T. curry powder	½ tsp. soy sauce
1 T. sugar	1 clove garlic, crushed
½ cup salad oil	2 T. Monteviña 1991 Fumé Blanc
2-3 lbs. boneless chicken breasts	

Marinade: In a bowl, stir together curry powder, sugar, oil, soy sauce, and wine. Set aside.

Skin chicken and cut into 3/4 inch cubes (for appetizer) or leave whole (for main course) and place in a plastic zip lock bag. Pour in marinade, seal bag, and refrigerate for two hours, turning occasionally.

Thread about 4 cubes of meat on small bamboo skewers and place on lightly greased grill. Cook skewers or chicken breasts until opaque in center. (Test to see.) Serve with almond sauce as a dipping or serving sauce.

Accompany with chilled bottle of 1991 Monteviña Fumé Blanc.

Almond Sauce: In a small pan, combine 1 cup water, 2 tablespoons Monteviña Fumé Blanc, 2/3 cup almond butter, and 2 cloves garlic, minced or pressed. Cook over medium heat until mixture boils and thickens. Remove from heat and stir in 2 tablespoons brown sugar, 1½ teaspoons lemon juice, 1 tablespoon soy sauce, and ½ teaspoon crushed red pepper. Let cool to room temperature before serving.

Amador Foothill Winery

12500 Steiner Road Plymouth, CA 95669
209/245-6307

Amador Foothill Winery was founded in 1980 and currently markets wines in fifteen states. The winery produces a Sauvignon Blanc/Semillon blend called Amador Fumé; a dry, crisp White Zinfandel with only 0.8% sugar; and their specialty—three single vineyard Zinfandels from vines ranging in age from 30 to 125 years. Sangiovese will be released for the first time in 1994.

Since production is limited to 10,000 cases per year, uncompromising attention is given to every detail of premium wine production. The clean, crisp white wines have an abundance of natural fruitiness to complement fish and fowl. The full flavored Zinfandels are great with lamb, pork, sausage and robust Italian dishes. Their colorful herb flower wine labels help link food and wine.

The owners/winemakers are the husband and wife team of Ben Zeitman and Katie Quinn. Ben was a former NASA chemist with thirteen years of home winemaking experience before founding Amador Foothill. Katie joined the winery in 1986 when they were married. She brought three years of experience at a Sonoma Valley winery and has a Master's degree in Oenology from UC Davis.

The tasting room is open without reservation weekends and most holidays from noon to five. Visitors are treated to a spectacular view of the Sierras. Picnic tables are available and informal tours of the vineyard and winery facility can be arranged with advance notice.

AMADOR FOOTHILL WINERY

Zin & Sage Grilled Game Hens

Marinade:

2 oz. Amador Foothill Zinfandel	3 T. fresh sage, chopped
3 cloves garlic, finely chopped	4 oz. olive oil
3 T. prepared Dijon-style mustard	6 game hens
1 T. black peppercorns, crushed	salt, as needed

Place wine, garlic, sage, pepper, and mustard in a bowl and mix with a whisk. Add oil slowly, in a steady stream, while whisking. The wine and oil will emulsify and thicken.

Cut the game hens along the backbone. Spread them and flatten by giving each a hard swat on the breastbone near the neck. Pour marinade mixture (reserve small amount for coating after cooking) over hens and marinate for 2 hours at room temperature, or overnight in the refrigerator.

To cook, grill over hot coals. Turn frequently to avoid burning. After the first turn, salt to taste. When done, place on serving plates and brush generously with marinade. Do not use the marinade which held the raw game hens. Garnish with sage sprigs. Serve with roasted new potatoes and barbecued corn.

The Foxes Bed & Breakfast Inn

PO Box 159 Sutter Creek, CA 95685
77 Main Street Sutter Creek
209/267-5882 Fax 209/267-0712

Pete and Min Fox purchased this 1857 home in 1979, opening the inn soon after offering one room accommodation only. Gradually they were able to offer three rooms. In 1986 a "Carriage House" was constructed next to the house, adding three more rooms with convenient off street parking below.

Three of these six rooms have wood burning fireplaces and three have TV tucked away in armoires. All are comfortably furnished using period antiques. Hospitality ranks first on the list of "musts" at Foxes with comfort and quality vying for second.

Breakfast is served on gleaming silver service to each room at your chosen time or in the garden when weather permits. Dining in the lovely English garden is a special treat for the yard is meticulously maintained so that even before spring arrives it is ablaze with everchanging color which continues through the fall.

Foxes have developed a reputation earning them a variety of coveted awards; number one in the Gold Country; top ten in California; top ten in Northern California; and a three star rating with Mobil.

Plan ahead. The inn is very popular and advance reservations are usually a necessity.

Foxes Special Eggs

1 cup half & half
1 T. butter
4 Large California Fresh Eggs
Pinch freshly ground black pepper
Dash cayenne pepper
2 T. shredded cheddar cheese
2 English muffins, halved and toasted

Heat the half & half with butter in non-stick frying pan. Slide eggs into the hot cream and keep separate. Sprinkle pepper over tops of eggs. When the whites begin to set, add the shredded cheese to each yolk. Finish cooking to desired doneness.

Place muffin halves on serving plate and top with eggs. Spoon hot cream mixture over top. Makes two servings.

Court Street Inn

215 Court Street Jackson, CA 95642
209/223-0416

The Court Street Inn is an elegant 1872 Victorian home located only two blocks from Jackson's famous Historic Main Street. The quiet, lovely residential area is graced by the loveliness of our inn. The inn is adorned by a large comfortable porch with beautiful wicker furniture and a cozy porch swing for those sweet moments of solitude or a romantic moment with a friend.

A brick courtyard separates the main house from the two bedroom cottage which is an exceptional addition to the facilities at The Court Street Inn. The cottage offers guests the convenience of their own living room with fireplace and a huge bathroom that has an old, but luxurious clawfoot tub. The interior of the main house is completely furnished in antiques that suit the mood and ambiance of the Inn.

All of our rooms hold either queen or king-sized beds. We offer you a cozy ambiance achieved by warm fireplaces, sunny sitting rooms, and a romantic woodstove or whirlpool tub for two.

Seafood Rings

8 hard cooked eggs
6 oz. crab meat, canned or fresh
¼ cup sour cream
1 tsp. lemon juice
1/3 cup butter
¼ lb. fresh mushrooms, sliced
1/3 cup flour
2 cups milk
½ cup chicken broth
¼ cup sherry
1 cup fresh uncooked shrimp
2 oz. jar sliced pimentos, drained
2 T. butter melted
½ cup dry bread crumbs

Heat oven to 350°. Slice eggs in half and mash yellows with fork. Add crab, sour cream and lemon juice. Blend well and refill egg white halves.

Melt 1/3 cup butter, add mushrooms; cook till softened. Stir in flour. Cook 1 minute till bubbly; gradually stir in milk, chicken broth, and sherry. Cook over medium heat till slightly thick and bubbly. Stir in shrimp and pimento.

Spoon about 1 cup sauce into 12 x 8 baking dish. Arrange eggs over sauce. Spoon remaining sauce over eggs. In a small bowl, combine 2 tablespoons butter and breadcrumbs. Sprinkle evenly over egg mixture. Bake for 20-25 minutes till bubbly. Let stand for 5 minutes.

Serve over twisted breadsticks previously baked.

Gate House Inn

1330 Jackson Gate Road Jackson, CA 95642 · 209/223-3500
One and one half miles north of the city of Jackson

Gate House is a charming turn-of-the-century Victorian offering its guests three elegant rooms and a luxurious two room suite, all with private baths. Each room is a huge step into our American past with dainty lace curtains, intricate handmade afghans, shiny brass and Early American queen size beds with Victorian furnishings to complete the comfortable decor.

Guests may relax on the wide homey porches or picnic on the lovely grounds; or enjoy an afternoon playing ping pong or lounging by the pool. A leisurely walk will take you past the historic Kennedy Mine Tailing Wheels and the rock formation from which Jackson Gate Road and our Inn derived their names. A short drive will take you to a grand selection of restaurants, wineries, and shopping.

A few short steps away from the main house is what we call our finest accommodation because of the privacy and intimacy of the very special bathroom. The furnishings include a romantic jacuzzi tub for two. This structure was the original caretaker's quarters and then became the summerhouse of the private residence.

Breakfast is served each morning at 9:00am in the formal dining room or you may prefer to eat in the privacy of your own lovely room.

Gate House Muffins

1 cup flour	1½ cups shredded carrots
1 cup Quick Quaker Oats	½ cup raisins
2 tsp. baking soda	2 large apples, shredded
1 tsp. baking powder	1 cup chopped nuts
½ tsp. salt	¼ cup oil
2 tsp. cinnamon	½ cup skim milk
1 cup brown sugar	2 eggs or 4 egg whites
1 tsp. vanilla	

Combine flour, oats, baking soda, baking powder, salt, cinnamon, and brown sugar. Then add carrots, raisins, apples, and nuts to dry ingredients and make a well in the center. Add the remaining ingredients and mix well until blended. Bake at 375° for 18-20 minutes in muffin tins.

The Wedgewood Inn

11941 Narcissus Road Jackson, CA 95642
209/296-4300 800/WEDGEWD(933-4393)

The Wedgewood Inn is tucked away on wooded acreage just ten minutes east of Jackson off Scenic Highway 88 in the Sierra foothills. This lovely country Victorian replica stirs memories of days-gone-by, yet provides the comfort of twentieth century living. Vic's stained glass and Jeannine's needlecraft work and Victorian lace lampshades are tastefully displayed throughout the inn which they have warmly furnished in European and American antiques.

On crisp, cool days the New England parlor stove glows with warmth. At other times, when the sun has worked hard, air conditioning cools and refreshes the inn.

The grounds are richly landscaped in English country style. Walking paths lead through the rose arbor to a Victorian gazebo in the garden. Rest on a bench near one of our sparkling fountains or just relax on the porch swing or in one of the hammocks. Croquet and horseshoes are available.

A full gourmet breakfast is graciously served on fine bone china in the formal dining room.

The Wedgewood Inn has been listed as one of the top 10 in "The Best of the Gold Country".

Eggs A La Wedgewood

Precook ½ to 1 pound chopped bacon until crisp; drain. Broccoli can replace bacon in this recipe.
12 eggs beaten with 1 tsp. nutmeg; add 3-4 tablespoons chopped fresh parsley. Mix together and scramble. Cool.

Layer the following in a greased quiche dish in lettered order:
a. Scrambled egg mixture
b. ½ cup sour cream
c. green onions, finely chopped
d. crisp fried bacon (or one cup blanched broccoli)
e. 12 (or more) fresh mushrooms
f. top generously with grated cheddar cheese
(Optional: refrigerate overnight)
Heat oven to 300°. Bake 20 minutes or until cheese is melted. Do not over bake.

Suggestion: Serve with Basil Buttered Tomatoes (Sliced tomatoes drizzled with melted butter and sprinkled with basil. Heat in microwave one minute. Do not cook. Serve on lettuce leaf.)

Amador Gold Country

St. George Hotel

PO Box 9 Volcano, CA 95689
#2 Main Street Volcano
209/296-4458

When the St. George Hotel was built in 1862 it was one of the most opulent hotels in the Mother Lode. It is currently in the Registry of Historic Buildings. This stately three story brick building has balconies along two sides and is elegantly covered with Virginia Creeper, Trumpet Vines, and fragrant Wisteria.

As with many historic hotels, the St. George boasts an old fashioned bar and dining room that welcomes guests, locals and international visitors. A special hit with guests is the immense lobby.

The original fourteen guest rooms have shared baths, and the six rooms in the annex each offer private baths.

Breakfast and dinner are served Wednesday through Sunday in the pleasant dining room which has a proper yesteryear look. Conference facilities for small groups (30-40) are available by prior notice.

Enjoy the history or our lovely hotel, relax in the grand back yard or take in some golf, tennis, skiing, fishing, or boating, all of which are close by.

Sillibub

3½ oz. wine* (4 oz. is ½ cup)
3 oz. sugar
1 oz. whipping cream
juice of one lemon

Whip all the ingredients together until dessert consistency (either rounded peaks or a bit more stiff). Serve in pretty glasses or parfaits.
*The best is Shenandoah Black Muscat!! But any will do.

Riding The Rivers of California's Gold Country

Karen Tenenbaum 1992

The golden grasses of the Sierra foothills hid their wealth until 1848, when John Marshall made the discovery that brought the Gold Rush of 1849 along the banks of the American River. The rivers of the area continue to erode their way to new deposits but as they do so they offer up adventure and fun for whitewater rafting enthusiasts of all ages.

Stanislaus River

Near Angels Camp
The Birthplace of California Whitewater
1 day, Class III, runs April-October

Bring the family back to the Stan to witness the river's power of renewal. Thought to be lost to the New Melones Reservoir in the winter of 1981-82, years of low rainfall have brought the swift waters of the nine-mile upper section of the Stanislaus back. Course through the deepest limestone canyon on the West Coast as a dozen memorable rapids continue to cleanse and rejuvenate. Marvel at the return of the sparkling beaches and wildflowers. Perhaps a symbol of what has been and what can be, the Stan's archaeological and historical sites are once again revealed. Be sentimental about the Stan. Those who have been come back again and again. Never been? Do it and you'll know why. Add a night in a charming B & B to a perfect day on the river. Gold country history, comfortable amenities and river adventure beckon.

Tuolumne River

Near Yosemite
1, 2, or 3 days, Class IV+, runs March-October
Take on your "Nemesis." Butt horns with "Ram's Head." Buck and swerve as you "Thread the Needle." Feel the shouts rise from your stomach as you descend into "Hell's Kitchen." This is it! The "Big T," California's "Wild and Scenic" star shining with explosive rapids and radiant scenic beauty.

American River

Near Placerville
1 to 2 days, Class III-IV, runs April-October
The South Fork of the American is California's most popular river run, and there are eight different ways to enjoy it. With options as diverse as Bed and Breakfast holidays, wilderness camping, hot air ballooning and action-packed jet-away adventures, special American River packages take the heart of whitewater excitement and surround it with unlimited opportunities for adventure and fun. Runs are also available on the North and Middle Forks of the American River.

Merced River

Near Yosemite
1 to 2 days, Class III-IV, runs April-July
You can hear the rush of tumbling spring water as the snow melts. You can see the orange poppies and redbuds blaze from the banks. The Merced, the jewel of the Sierra is back for its yearly run, winning the crown as California's favorite springtime river. Free-flowing and calm through Yosemite National Park, just beyond the valley floor the river picks up power and heads toward the Gold Country. The Merced is an absolute must.

Where the World Is Always Saturday
More really is better

Some say spending just a day on the river will make you fall in love with its magic. They say the scenery is breath-taking and the sky is its original blue. They describe the powerful rapids that meet you and renew you and send you back into that other world clear and refreshed. And they're right.

But imagine more than one day on the river. Imagine you don't have to be back to your other life tomorrow and how good that knowledge makes today feel. It's like today is always Saturday, and Monday is always the day after tomorrow.

Consider O.A.R.S. multiple-day river trips as endless Saturdays in a world of great

Gold Country Pottage

Serve 6
Preparation time: 1¾ hours
This wonderful soup will warm your body and soothe your soul after a day on the river.

¾ cup lentils
¾ cup split peas
¾ cup barley
6 large carrots, chopped
Two 6 oz. cans of tomato paste

2 yellow onions, sliced
3 large potatoes, diced
6 garlic cloves, chopped
3 bay leaves

salt, pepper, basil, oregano, dill seed, and celery seed to taste

The morning before this soup is to be served, place lentils and peas in a jar with water. That evening, pour lentils and peas with water into a large pot. Add barley, carrots, onions, potatoes, garlic, bay leaves, and salt. Add enough water to cover all vegetables amply. Cover pot and bring to a boil. Cook at a high simmer 45 minutes. Stir in tomato paste, pepper, and herbs. Cook another 30 minutes at a low simmer. Serve with Parmesan cheese as topping. This is also wonderful with a tablespoon or two of sherry in each bowl.

beauty, adventure and relaxation. Here a child sees her first eagle and learns the names of cave dwellers. Here friends new and old work together to meet rapids head-on, then reflect on their accomplishments in the moonlit wilderness. Here generations of families rediscover each other on lazy drifts and sandy beaches and in pristine campsites where the food is mouth-watering and the conversation one-of-a-kind. And here, for lovers, there is always tomorrow.

So come to the river. Come for just a day and get a taste of its magic. Come to the river with your friends and family to be reawakened and renewed. Then consider O.A.R.S. multiple-day river trips as endless Saturdays. These are the best days of your life. Spend them with O.A.R.S.
209/736-4677 or 800/446-RAFT

Calaveras Gold Country

Photo from color print by Dick James

Calaveras Gold Country Map

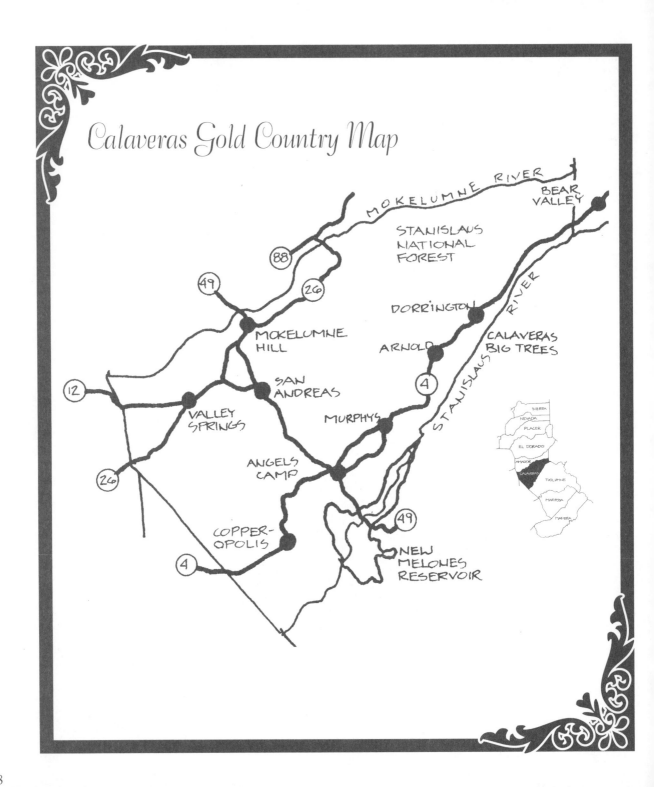

Calaveras Gold Country Wine Map

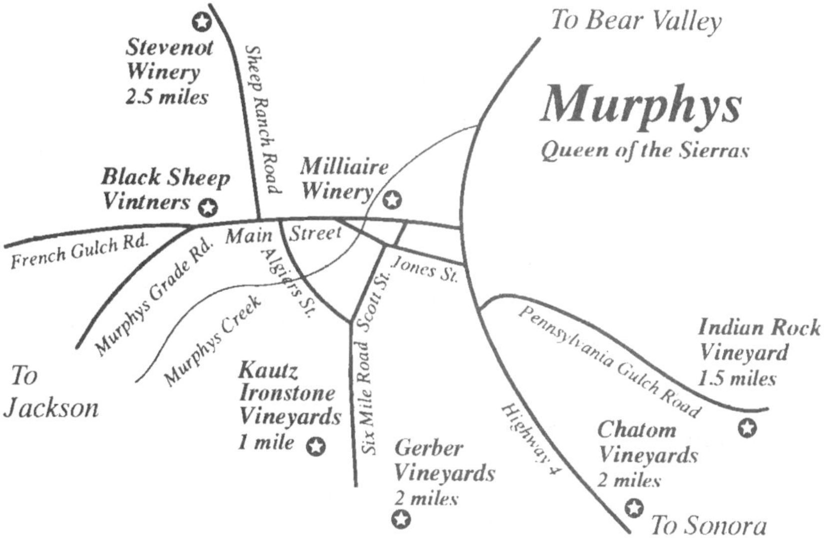

Stevenot Winery 2.5 miles

Sheep Ranch Road

Black Sheep Vintners

Milliaire Winery

To Bear Valley

Murphys
Queen of the Sierras

French Gulch Rd. *Main Street*

Murphys Grade Rd. *Algiers St.*

Jones St.

Murphys Creek

Six Mile Road *Scott St.*

Pennsylvania Gulch Road

Indian Rock Vineyard 1.5 miles

To Jackson

Kautz Ironstone Vineyards 1 mile

Gerber Vineyards 2 miles

Highway 4

Chatom Vineyards 2 miles

To Sonora

CALAVERAS
WINE
ASSOCIATION

IRONSTONE VINEYARDS

BLACK SHEEP VINTNERS

Black Sheep Winery
209/728-2157
Open weekends 12 to 5 and by appointment

Kautz Ironstone Vineyards
209/728-1251
Open daily 11 to 5

Chatom Vineyards

MILLIAIRE

Chatom Vineyards
209/736-6500
Open daily 11 to 4:30

Milliaire Vineyard Selections
209/728-1658
Open daily 11 to 4:30

INDIAN ROCK VINEYARD

Stevenot

Stevenot Winery
209/728-3436
Open daily 10 to 5

Indian Rock Vineyard
209/728-2266
Open weekends & holidays 11 to 5 & by appointment

Gerber Vineyards

For information, call 800/225-3764

Calaveras Gold Country

24 Hour Visitor Information and direct access to lodging and recreational facilities 800/225-3764

Murphys Queen of the Sierra

The beautiful, picturesque village of Murphys known for its uncountable natural attractions, friendly merchants and unique shops, wineries, art galleries, gold panning, golf and river rafting trips was settled in 1848 by the Murphy boys, Daniel and John. From a small tent the Murphy brothers did some very shrewd trading. They used the local Indians for labor on their claims and sold supplies to them at inflated prices. I don't know how he got away with it, but one of them even married the chief's daughter. Both boys were millionaires before they turned twenty five.

Fifteen miles up the mountain, A.T. Dowd put Calaveras on the international map when he discovered the large grove of Sequoia Redwoods. The giant redwoods quickly grew in fame and the Sperry & Perry Hotel, now known as Murphys Historic Hotel & Lodge, was built in Murphys in 1855 to accommodate the travelers. The old hotel register contains names such as Mark Twain, Horatio Alger, Ulysses S. Grant, and Charles Bolton, a.k.a. Black Bart the "Gentleman Bandit". The current register contains some pretty famous people, too.

The Murphys area has a climate that closely imitates that of some wine regions in France. There are now six wineries that have staked their claim within a four mile radius of Murphys Main Street.

Just 9 miles east of Angels Camp off Highway 4 and offering all the amenities you desire for your entire family including lodging in a famous historic hotel or bed & breakfast inn, Murphys remains a favorite place to get away from it all.

Angels and Amphibians

Angels Camp, like Murphys, was named for a shopkeeper, Henry Angel of Rhode Island who started a trading post there in 1848.

Several good strikes were made by early miners and within the year over 4,000 miners were working the surface gold of Angels. The source of gold played out quickly but hardrock mining kept the gold industry flourishing until recently.

In 1864, Mark Twain wrote his first successful short story, *The Celebrated Jumping Frog of Calaveras County* and Angels Camp became linked with frogs apparently for all time. The Jumping Frog Jubilee is held here annually the third weekend in May.

Angels Camp is today a busy little town of 3,000. You must not miss the fabulous mining museum located on Main Street (Highway 49). The indoor and outdoor exhibits of mining equipment and memorabilia will give you a true picture of the days of the Gold Rush.

San Andreas

San Andreas came into being sometime during the winter of 1848 when a small group of miners started working claims where the town now stands. The *Gringos* arrived in larger numbers and the two groups lived together in something less than harmony.

Two names keep popping up in connection with San Andreas whenever it is mentioned. It is sometimes difficult to determine where history ends and legend begins, so let's just jump in and forget accuracy.

Although the name crops up frequently in California history, Joaquin Murietta seems to be mentioned most frequently in this area. Sonora also claims that he first fell afoul of the law on their side of the river. There is even a story about him showing up at one of the Swedish homesteads in Kingsburg, about one hundred and fifty miles from San Andreas. (Since I heard this one from my grandmother it must be true.) Clearly some of these reports are untrue and every Mexican bandit must have been named Joaquin, or that delinquent child had an awfully fast horse.

The story goes that Joaquin was driven off his claim by greedy *Gringos*. This actually happened all the time, so we have little reason to doubt this part of the story. In some versions, his beautiful young wife was raped and murdered by Yankee miners. He then proceeded to terrorize the whole Mother Lode, robbing the rich, giving to the poor, becoming a legend in his own time.

Joaquin, along with his partner Three Fingered Jack, came to a bloody end at the hand of lawman Harry Love. Jack's hand with three fingers and Joaquin's head were pickled up in jars and displayed wherever people were interested in art and culture.

Black Bart is more firmly grounded in history. Although his nefarious deeds took place twenty years after the initial Gold Rush, he has earned his place in the region's history.

Black Bart, the most famous highwayman of the era, was always on foot, dressed in a linen duster with a flour sack over his head. He carried a shotgun and a blanket with an axe rolled inside to crack open the strongboxes which were handed over without a fight. He is known to have committed 28 stagecoach robberies between 1877 and 1883.

Always a gentleman, he never harmed drivers or passengers. It was later revealed that Bart didn't own a single shell for his gun. He sometimes left bits of verse signed "Black Bart, PO8".

During one of the robberies he dropped a handkerchief with a laundry mark which was traced to San Francisco and one of its leading citizens, Charles E. Bolton. Charles E. Bolton was actually Charles E. Boles, a shipping clerk originally from Illinois. He had developed a taste for the good life and found a way to finance some of the finer things.

The newspapers had a field day when Bart/ Charles was tried in San Andreas. His exploits, wealth, cunning, and literary skills were all greatly exaggerated and turned into the stuff of legends. Bart spent six years in San Quentin and then disappeared into the San Joaquin Valley.

San Andreas is now the county seat of Calaveras County and still has a wild west flair, especially on Main Street. The old courthouse where Black Bart was held and tried is now the county museum. Be sure to look for the sign, 'Black Bart slept here'.

Mokelumne Hill

All the mining towns were rough places. It's hard to imagine a more volatile combination than gold, booze, racial tension, women of easy virtue, and young men, often with more brawn than brains. Every settlement had its share of murder and mayhem but Mokelumne Hill probably had more than any other town in the Mother Lode.

Founded in 1848, 'Moke Hill' was among the richest of the digs. Claims in some areas were confined to 16 square feet and many fortunes were made.

Just south of town in Chile Gulch, Dr. Concha worked his claim with slave labor from Chile. This resulted in the Americans initiating legal action which quickly escalated into all out war. Several men died, and Washington, D.C. and Santiago Chile became involved before it was over.

The French Wars started two years later when the French miners raised the Tri-color over their claims. The Americans attacked, motivated more by greed than national pride.

The gold played out and Moke Hill shrunk from 15,000 to less than the 600 who live there today. But Moke Hill is well worth a stop. Many of the original buildings are still in place and an air of true authenticity exists. Ask at the Hotel Léger about the ghosts of the town; the stampede of ghostly cattle; the sobbing of a little child; and more.

Hotel Léger Est. 1851

PO Box 50 Mokelumne Hill, CA 95245 · 8304 Main Street Mokelumne Hill
2 blocks east of Highway 49 between San Andreas and Jackson
209/286-1401 or 800/225-3764 ext.335

Over one hundred years ago, George Léger came from Europe to the Gold Rush boom town of Mokelumne Hill and built a unique hotel. It soon became a Mother Lode landmark, famous throughout the West for its service and hospitality.

The spirit lives on at the Hotel Léger today. Now a Bed & Breakfast Inn, it is a delightful combination of Gold Country nostalgia and modern comfort; a place for those who want an unusual experience.

'Moke Hill' is tucked away from the tourist areas, but is only fifteen minutes to one hour from gold panning, spelunking, river rafting, and skiing. Enjoy one of the thirteen rooms decorated with

antiques. Be whisked away to another time when you become a character or sleuth in a murder mystery set in the 1880's. "Murder in the Mother Lode" is held once monthly.

Nonno's Restaurant at Hotel Léger serves up authentic family style dinners Thursday through Sunday. While visiting, enjoy the old Frontier Style Saloon or lounge around the pool. Banquet facilities are available in the Courthouse Theatre.

All rooms are non-smoking. Group, senior, and corporate rates are offered Sunday through Thursday and children are welcome.

Linguini con Vongoli alla Mario

20 oz. linguini	¼ cup dry white wine
6 tsp. dry basil	3 T. olive oil
¼ cup lemon juice	½ cup Parmesan cheese
6 T. fresh parsley, chopped	
Six 10 oz. cans whole baby clams, drained	

Cook and drain pasta. Sauté parsley, basil, wine, lemon juice and olive oil. Reduce by half. Reheat pasta in boiling water for a few seconds and drain. Combine sautéed ingredients, pasta, and clams. Toss lightly with Parmesan cheese. Serve and enjoy.

Black Bart Inn

PO Box 216 San Andreas, Ca 95247
55 West St. Charles Street San Andreas
209/754-3808 800/225-3764 ext. 331

The relaxed and warm atmosphere of the Black Bart Inn is a genuine reflection of an era and a way of life that has almost disappeared from today's scene. It represents a fascinating way to relax and enjoy your valuable leisure time. And it is the fun spot of the Mother Lode.

Black Bart Inn invites you to inquire about special banquets for clubs and organizations, and about their splendid mini-conference facilities.

Excellent accommodations are yours at the Black Bart Inn, your home away from home... and enjoy seeing some of the most historic country in California.

Be sure to visit the historic County Courthouse and jail where stagecoach bandit Black Bart was held. There are three nearby caves to tour and golf is good at nearby La Contenta Golf & Country Club, a professional layout of 18 great holes.

"You are the guest at Black Bart Inn and we treat you that way!"

Linguini With Clam Sauce

One 12oz. package of linguine
3 cloves garlic, finely chopped
2 T. olive oil
½ cube butter
½ cup cream
4 T. parsley, minced
½ cup Parmesan cheese, grated
2 cans minced clams

Cook linguine as directed. Sauté garlic in oil and butter. Add clams and cream. Toss with noodles. Stir in parsley and cheese. Season with salt and pepper. Serves four to six. Serve with a chilled white wine, green salad and French bread.

The real secret of this recipe is to have fresh clams. Just how this is accomplished, I will not divulge... Happy Diggin!

Editor's note: In June 1980 this recipe earned Don a well deserved claim to fame outside of the Mother Lode. He was honored as a "Chef of the West" by Sunset Magazine.

Courtyard Bed & Breakfast

334 West St. Charles Street San Andreas, CA 95249
209/754-1518 800/225-3764 ext. 332

Courtyard Bed & Breakfast is a comfortable 75 year old home nestled in the Gold Rush territory and exhibiting lovely gardens and impressive rock formations. The master suite boasts a baby grand piano, a walk-in closet, a toasty fireplace, its own private bath, and elegant French doors leading out to the hot tub and landscaped deck.

A 400 year old California Live Oak tree lives in the Courtyard. Coffee is served in your room in the morning on a silver service and hot breakfast follows under the trees in the garden, weather permitting.

Lacy Potato Cakes

2 large baking potatoes, grated
1 egg
2 T. flour
1 large clove garlic
½ tsp. salt
½ tsp. pepper
¼ cup toasted pecans

Chop pecans in medium sized chunks and bake at 350° until toasted. Mix egg, garlic, salt, pepper, and flour in mixing bowl. Stir in grated potatoes and fry in 3 tablespoons oil until golden brown; turn and fry other side until crispy. Serve any egg dish as an accompaniment.

Raspberry Bread Pudding with Raspberry Syrup

Cube 4 slices of thick white bread. (I use Texas Toast.) Place ½ of the cubes in the bottom of a buttered baking dish (8 x 8) and cover with 1½ cups frozen raspberries. Top with remaining bread cubes.

In a mixing bowl mix together:
5 eggs
¾ cup evaporated milk
½ cup sugar
1 tsp vanilla

Pour over to coat all bread cubes. Cover with foil and refrigerate over night. Bake at 350° for 1 hour. Remove foil and place under broiler briefly until golden brown.

Combine 1 cup syrup with ½ cup raspberries and heat in microwave for one minute. Serve piping hot with link sausages and fresh fruit.

Cooper House Bed & Breakfast Inn

Calaveras Gold Country

PO Box 1388 Angels Camp, CA 95222
1184 Church Street Historic Angels Camp,
One block east of Main Street · 800/225-3764 ext. 326 or 209/736-2145

In 1988 Angels Camp's first Bed & Breakfast Inn, the Cooper House, received an architectural award for restoration of an historic building. Just a block from the historic downtown on a quiet side street, it is invisible from the main thoroughfare. The Inn is surrounded by shade trees and manicured gardens making it a delightful place to relax and enjoy afternoon refreshments.

The house is a Craftsman style bungalow. A graceful redwood walk curves up to the inviting veranda which overlooks the garden path winding down to the gazebo. The rich oak windowed door opens directly into our gracious living room with its high ceilings and magnificent greenstone fireplace. Our three spacious suites, each with private bath, were professionally decorated to recall the Craftsman period.

This quaint environment takes you back in time, although modern air conditioned comfort pampers you. Whether your visit is for business or pleasure, staying at the Cooper House is a special experience. A full country breakfast is served each morning on your private patio, in the dining room, or in the privacy of your own room.

Cooper House Parmesan Eggs

1 T. butter
2 T. Parmesan cheese
2 whole eggs
dash salt, pepper & fresh nutmeg

Coat the bottom of a buttered soufflé dish with shredded Parmesan cheese. Break two whole eggs on top of the cheese. Sprinkle the eggs with salt, pepper, and fresh nutmeg; dollop with butter. Bake at 325 degrees for about 12 minutes and garnish with fresh chopped chives.

Kautz Ironstone Vineyards

PO Box 2263 Murphys, CA. 95247 · 209/728-1251 Fax 209/728-1275
1¾ miles from Murphys Historic Hotel & Lodge

You've been drinking wines from Ironstone grapes for years, but hidden under some of those famous Napa and Sonoma labels. The John Kautz family has enjoyed the reputation of being growers of high quality wine grapes for over 20 years.

At Ironstone Vineyards, winery, and caverns, visitors will step back in time to the days of Black Bart and Mark Twain as they walk the same trails through the oak and pines, lakes, apple orchards, amphitheater and vineyards. The concept for this incredible facility makes it the perfect site for weddings, concerts and other special group events.

The Winery and Visitors Tour Center covers 1 2/3 acres and stands seven stories above the huge redwood doors that guard the 10,000 square foot aging cavern.

The aging cavern encompasses a majestic network of six caves. Though there are many natural caverns in the Murphys area, some of which are well known tourist attractions, only the Ironstone caves are man-made. The cavern was not only created for the main and necessary purpose of aging wines; with the addition of the waterfall and the music rotunda, the caves also offer a unique experience in dining and entertaining.

For those of you who remember the controversial Sacramento Alhambra Theater, you will be delighted to know that a large piece of its history, the beautiful pipe organ, is alive and well, and residing on the fifth floor at the Ironstone complex.

Call about our newsletter which will keep you updated on our calendar of concerts and other public events. You are invited to visit our beautiful winery, tasting room, and unique caverns daily from 11:00am to 5:00pm.

Ravioli di Zucca

(Recipe contributed by Mark Casale, head chef at Caffe Donatello in Sacramento)

Filling:
1 large butternut squash, peeled and cut into large cubes
¼ cup chopped walnuts
2 T. chopped fresh sage (1 T. dry sage)
1 lb. ricotta
1 egg
¼ cup grated Parmesan
Salt & pepper to taste

Sauce:
½ oz. dry mushrooms (soak in warm water for 15 minutes)
2 oz. sliced mushrooms
¼ cup Kautz Ironstone Chardonnay
2 oz. cold butter
2 T. olive oil

Roast squash in 350° oven until browned and soft (about 20-25 minutes). Mash squash; blend in other ingredients. Fill fresh pasta sheets with filling. Cut into desired shapes.
While ravioli are cooking (3 minutes fresh; 6 minutes frozen), sauté mushrooms in olive oil; add Chardonnay, cook until almost dry. Whisk in butter (off flame). Toss in pasta. Serve with grated Parmesan.

Black Sheep Vintners

PO Box 1851, Murphys, CA 95247
West end of Murphys at Murphys Grade Road
Phone & Fax 209/728-2157

Take Murphys Grade Road a short and beautiful few miles east of Angels Camp and as you enter the historic tree lined village of Murphys your attention will be caught by the rustic barn that houses Black Sheep Winery where you can enjoy tasting amongst the barrels of aging wines.

The winemakers and proprietors, Dave and Jan Olson, are deeply committed to using only Sierra Foothill grapes. "Our wine is really chosen in the vineyard. The location and soil of the vineyard will dictate much of the style and Mother Nature's weather patterns will affect the grapes from year to year" says Dave Olson. Dave guides the wine, choosing French or American oak barrels and so forth to enhance the way the wine wants to be. Wines by Black Sheep Vintners include their awarding winning Zinfandel, Cabernet Sauvignon, Chardonnay, Sauvignon Blanc, and True Frogs Lily Pad White, their whimsical frog label.

Those of you who have not experienced Calaveras Wine Country are in for a treat. You will be delighted to find a relaxed atmosphere, few crowds, pleasant wine hosts and good wines.

Basque Leg of Lamb with Mushroom and Wine Sauce

One 5-6 lb. leg of lamb	salt and pepper to taste
6 cloves garlic, peeled	2 T. olive oil

Heat oven to 400°. Poke six holes in the fat side of the lamb and insert cloves of garlic. Rub the entire roast with salt and pepper and a small amount of oil. Use meat thermometer in thickest part of leg. Place in a roasting pan with rack and roast for 40 minutes to brown meat. Turn oven to 325° and continue cooking for another 40 to 50 minutes or until the thermometer reads 140°.

Black Sheep Zinfandel and Mushroom Sauce

2 cups beef stock	2 T. cornstarch mixed in ¼ cup water
1 cup Black Sheep Zinfandel	1 bay leaf
2 T. olive oil	½ tsp. dried thyme, whole
2 cloves garlic, crushed	Salt and pepper to taste
¾ pound mushrooms, sliced	½ tsp. mint (optional)

Simmer beef stock and wine in a 2 quart sauce pan. Sauté garlic in olive oil; add mushrooms, bay leaf, and thyme. Sauté until mushrooms are tender. Add cornstarch mixture and simmer until thick. Add salt and pepper to taste and mint during last 10 minutes. Serve over roast lamb.

Dunbar House, 1880
Bed & Breakfast Inn

PO Box 1375 Murphys, CA 95247 · 271 Jones Street Murphys
One block from historic Murphys Main Street
209/728-2897 800/225-3764 ext 321 Fax 209/728-1451

Arrive at the Inn and begin a visit with history. From the moment you walk through the gate, you are treated with old fashioned courtesy. The afternoon appetizer buffet, the wine chilling in your room, the sweet symphony music filling the halls, the beautiful silver and crystal, the small signs of someone from another era having just left the room— all of this has to be experienced.

The guest rooms each have private baths, queen beds with down comforters, wood burning stoves, and a TV & VCR with a classic film library for your enjoyment. All rooms are supplied with a refrigerator, hair dryer, and cassette player, and are beautifully decorated to match the 1880 Italianate ambiance.

Our Cedar Suite offers up its own sun porch with day bed and a two person whirlpool bath, champagne, and a towel warmer.

A full country breakfast is served each morning. You may choose to eat privately in your room, with other guests in the dining room, or, in pleasant weather, amongst the flora of the elegant inn gardens.

Spinach, Sausage & Potato Crust Quiche

Crust:

24 oz. pkg thawed hash browned potatoes   1/3 cup melted butter

Squeeze any excess moisture from potatoes; mix potatoes with melted butter and press mixture into a 10 inch pie pan. (Use 9 inch pie plate to press and form crust). Bake at 425° for 25 minutes. Set aside.

Filling: (Decrease oven to 375°)

½ lb bulk sausage   3 eggs, mixed
¼ cup chopped onion   1½ cups half & half cream
1 clove garlic, minced   2 T. Parmesan cheese
1½ cups shredded Monterey Jack cheese   Paprika
One 10 oz. pkg frozen, chopped spinach, cooked & drained

In a skillet cook the sausage, green onion, and garlic; drain. Add the spinach and the stuffing mix. Sprinkle the Monterey Jack cheese, then the sausage mixture into the shell. In a bowl, combine the eggs and half & half; pour over the sausage. Bake in a 375° oven for 45 minutes. Sprinkle with Parmesan and paprika. Bake 15 minutes longer or until a knife inserted in the center comes out clean. Let stand 15 minutes before cutting and serving.

Murphys Historic Hotel & Lodge

PO Box 329 Murphys, CA 95247 · Main Street Murphys
7 miles east of Highway 49 Angels Camp. Take Murphys Grade Road direct to
Main Street or take Highway 4 and turn left at the Business District sign.
800/532-7684 209/728-3444 Fax 209/728-1590

In the very heart of Murphys is the picturesque old hotel whose register reads like a historical "Who's Who". Murphys was the natural overnight stage stop on a trip from San Francisco via Stockton by river steamer and by train to Milton where the tourists would take Matteson's Stage and arrive in Murphys around dinner time. Reading the names of the famous and notorious people who signed the old hotel register gives you an idea of the world wide interest in the Calaveras Grove of Big Trees in the late 1800s.

Not only is the Murphys Hotel a wonderful place to stay while visiting Calaveras Wine Country but it is also the optimum choice for conferences and seminars, as well as reunions and weddings.

Summer packages include golf, river rafting, theatre evenings and more. Winter packages also include skiing and snowmobiling.

The hotel's complete guest services include accommodations, dining room, saloon, conference/banquet areas and horse drawn carriage rides.

Murphys Hotel Crab Cakes

1 lb. crab meat, well drained	¼ cup chives, chopped
¼ cup mayonnaise	1½ oz. extra strong Dijon-style mustard
1 oz. lemon juice	1 egg
2 oz. Worchestershire sauce	¼ cup sourdough bread crumbs

Mix above ingredients; form into ½ inch thick 3 oz. cakes. Cook in clarified butter at medium to medium high until golden brown on both sides.
Serve with lemon and tartar sauce.

The Redbud Inn

PO Box 716 Murphys, CA 95247
402 Main Street Murphys
209/728-8533 800/827-8533 Fax 209/728-9123

The Redbud Inn is the first new inn to be built in 136 years in historic Murphys "Queen of the Sierra". It offers 11 spacious rooms, most with private balconies, woodstoves or fireplaces, and spa tubs. Breakfast will be served in the bay windowed dining room adjoining the living room where evening wine and hors d'oeuvres are served in front of the huge stone fireplace.

Located in old style "Miner's Exchange" on historic Murphys Main Street, guests may visit the many fine shops, picnic in the park, attend plays at our Black Bart Playhouse, listen to music at a gourmet coffee house, sample award winning local wines, enjoy a candlelight dinner or a hotdog on a park bench. All of this within a three block radius.

An adjoining conference center can accommodate groups of 30 to 40 for meetings and celebrations. Special tours of local caverns, wineries and historic sites can be arranged by the innkeepers as well as river rafting trips and guided hikes with a professional photographer, an historian, or a botanist.

The Redbud Inn is scheduled to open in July of 1993.

Yam Patties

2 cups grated yam	1 tsp. lemon pepper
1 beaten egg	1 tsp. salt (to taste-we like 'em salty)
1½ T. flour	½ tsp. (or more) cayenne (we also like 'em hot!)

Mix well and fry dollar size patties in hot oil till browned on both sides. Drain on paper towels. Serve warm with your choice of drinks.

The Trade Carriage House

PO Box 2429 Murphys, CA 95247 · 600 Algiers Street Murphys
One and one half block from Murphys Main Street
209/728-3909 evenings 800/800-3408 days

When you stay at The Trade Carriage House you enjoy the comforts of home, including a well equipped kitchen at your disposal. The two bedroom cottage is furnished with wicker and antiques, and has a cozy, relaxing atmosphere. Experience indoor and outdoor dining on the private veranda, or walk to a local restaurant. the house is well situated less than two blocks from historic Murphys Main Street, where you will find unique shops, wineries, art galleries and more.

When available, a horse drawn carriage ride will be provided. Please inquire.

Cynthia's Eggplant Marinara

Fry sliced eggplant in olive oil until tender and place in lasagna pan (single layer). Spoon marinara sauce over it and add mozzarella and grated Parmesan cheese. Bake until hot and bubbly.

Cynthia's Garlic Bread

Smash fresh chopped garlic; add fresh or dry basil and spread over bread. Put into damp paper bag and cook at 350° until very hot.

The Historic Avery Hotel

PO Box 371 Avery, CA 95224 · 4573 Moran Road Avery
Located on Moran Road in Avery; off Scenic Highway 4; sixteen miles east of Angels Camp
and twenty six miles west of Bear Valley Ski Area. · 800/225-3764 ext 316 209/795-9935 Fax 209/795-5763

In its early history the Avery Hotel was known as the "Half Way House". It was the stopping off place between the gold fields of Murphys and Calaveras Big Trees. The farmhouse style structure was built in 1850 by Joe Goodall as a residence for his family. A few years later, Peter Avery and his wife Nancy became the owners and inn-keepers.

Today the spirit of the independent pioneer continues with Phyllis Gotelli, her son Mike and daughter Sherrie Lockhart.

This family purchased the hotel in the spring of 1992 and have restored it to its original splendor and more.

Enjoy the country farmhouse porch over looking the restful lawn garden where brunch is served on Sundays when weather permits and a Dixieland band plays on the first Sunday of each month.

Beautiful gold rush era rooms, an elegant turn of the century dining room, and an old fashioned saloon make this a trip worth taking.

Crab Crepes with Curried Gruyere Sauce

20-22 of your favorite crepes
Sauté 4 bunches chopped green onion & 4 or 5 chopped celery ribs in butter until soft. Cool slightly. Add 2 egg whites and stir. Set aside.

Add 1½ cups flour to 6 tablespoons melted butter and cook until bubbly for 3 minutes, being careful not to let it brown. Add 1½ cups milk and cook until thickened (about 3 minutes). Cool slightly. Add 2 egg whites and stir. Set aside.

Put both in large bowl. Combine with 1½ pounds well drained fresh crab, ¾ cup seasoned breadcrumbs, 2 tablespoons finely chopped fresh parsley, 1/8 teaspoon cayenne pepper, ¼ teaspoon ground white pepper and 1/3 teaspoon salt. Mix well. Add more bread crumbs if too thin too roll. Heap down the center of crepe and roll.

Spread on pan sprayed with Pam and bake for 10 to 15 minutes in a 350° oven. Or cover 2 crepes with plastic wrap and microwave on high for 2 minutes. Cover with Curried Gruyere Sauce. Sprinkle with fresh chopped parsley and paprika.

Curried Gruyere Sauce
Melt 8 tablespoons butter. Add 1½ cups flour; cook until bubbly for 3 minutes. Add 2 cups milk and one quart heavy whipping cream. Bring to a boil over medium heat, stirring frequently. Add 2 tablespoons chicken bouillon granules or soup base, 1½ teaspoon curry, 1/8 teaspoon cayenne pepper, 2 or 3 dashes white pepper, and 1½ cups shredded Gruyere cheese. Stir and continue cooking to melt well. Serve over crepes (or fresh steamed vegetables).

The Dorrington Hotel

PO Box 4307 Dorrington, CA 95223 · 3431 Scenic Highway 4 Dorrington
Approximately 20 miles east of Murphys and 29 miles east of
Angels Camp · 209/795-5800 800/225-3764 ext.312

Built in 1860 by John and Rebecca Gardner, the Dorrington Hotel was a stage coach stop on the Big Trees-Carson Valley Road which was a toll road from 1862 to 1910. The hotel served as a depot for stockmen and as a summer resort for international guests visiting Calaveras Big Trees.

Noted for its ice cold spring, it was called Cold Spring Ranch until the establishment of a U.S. Post Office. Rebecca's maiden name was submitted to the postal department and the town has been known as Dorrington since 1902.

Over the years, occupants of the historic inn have often had reason to believe in the old but persistent legend that Rebecca's ghost still haunts the old hostelry.

Today the hotel has been restored to provide a gracious and relaxed atmosphere. Cozy handmade quilts, brass beds, and handsome antiques fill the five guest rooms. Fresh fruit and other amenities will make you feel at home.

In the morning, a full breakfast with freshly ground gourmet coffee and a newspaper will be served in the dining room.

Enjoy a tastefully prepared meal in the casual elegance of the Northern Italian style restaurant or soak up the sun and fresh air on the summer patio overlooking pines and meadows.

Little Pizzas

1 small can chopped olives
1 small can chopped green chilis
1 clove garlic, chopped
4 green onions, chopped
1¼ cups grated cheddar cheese
1 small can tomato paste
1/3 cup oil

Mix all ingredients together. Sprinkle in a little thyme, oregano, and salt. Put on rye rounds and heat in 350° oven for about 10 minutes.

Jensen's Pick & Shovel Ranch

*T*he experience of prospecting for gold is often more therapeutic than it is profitable. And two of the most down-to-earth "therapists" you will ever meet are owner Margie Jensen and miner Jess Keller at Jensen's Pick & Shovel Ranch near Angels Camp and Murphys in Calaveras County. Take Scenic Highway 4 east of Angels Camp about 4 miles to Parrotts Ferry Road. Turn right and approximately one half mile past Moaning Cavern Road you will see signs for Jensen's Pick & Shovel Ranch on your left.

Here you can take gold prospecting as seriously as your imagination and your physical hardiness will let you. Margie Jensen offers tours with experienced guides who teach visitors everything they need to know before heading out on their own.

Tours can range from two hours on a corner of the ranch or a few hours on the Stanislaus River to extensive prospecting trips where you raft to or are dropped in by helicopter to areas that are inaccessible by car and too far on foot.

Over half the ranch is made up of patented mining claims and many examples of early prospecting adventures can still be seen on the property. Visitors will also see evidence of the Mi-

Wuk Indians that inhabited this area. Some fine examples of Indian grinding rocks are seen in several locations on the ranch and often such things as arrow heads, beads, shells and tools have been found on the property.

Your very own mining equipment, from pans to sluices, and other gold related items including jewelry, are for sale in the museum-like tour room. Brochures highlighting adventures you can experience all over the area make it a wonderful visitors center, too.

When asked about her attraction to gold prospecting and the concept of offering the expeditions to families, Margie responded, "It's not the money. It's the challenge of reading the land; finding a spot and proving that gold is really there. It is the way the children's faces light up when they find a little gold. And I mean children of all ages. Even if we struck it rich, we would just give it away anyway, so this way everyone can enjoy the experience."

This statement pretty much says it all about the atmosphere at Jensen's Pick & Shovel Ranch. They are the nicest people around and their attitude typifies the hospitality that reigns in California's Gold Country.

For more information on gold prospecting call 209/736-0287 or 800/225-3764 ext 27.

Caverns of California's Gold Country

Under the gently rolling hills of Calaveras and Tuolumne Counties, hidden from summer sun and winter's blast are nearly one hundred limestone caverns. These are almost all well kept secrets known only to the small group of cavers or spelunkers in the area. The caves

are extremely fragile and damage done to them is irreparable. Damage to the caver is also irreparable if he or she doesn't know what they are doing.

Fortunately, in Calaveras County you don't have to be an experienced caver or be privy to secrets to explore beautiful caverns. The enthusiastic staff at Moaning Cavern and California Caverns will take you on tours, letting you safely explore the underground wonderland of the limestone caverns.

The caverns are formed in a type of limestone known as marble. Geological forces compressed lime bearing algae which had settled to the bottom of the sea into limestone and then marble. The caverns began as hot springs with volcanic gasses dissolving into the water. Hydrogen sulfide and carbon dioxide rose to the surface reacting with surface water forming sulfuric acid which dissolved the limestone. The water eventually drained away, leaving the caverns.

After the water drained away, the formations began to grow. Rain water and outside moisture combine with carbon dioxide to form carbonic acid. The acid is absorbed into the ground and dissolves limestone. When this dissolved limestone reaches the air inside the caves it releases carbon dioxide and leaves crystals of calcite. Stalactites are formed when calcite is deposited on the ceiling and stalagmites are formed when it is deposited on the floors. Sometimes you will see where a stalactite and a stalagmite have joined to form a column. The distinctive drapery formations are caused when water runs along a wall and deposits calcite in a ribbon.

Moaning Cavern

At Moaning Cavern you will be led down the well-lit marble passages into California's largest public cavern chamber. Amazing shapes and figures cling to the walls and ceilings in this treasure house of natural statuary.

A one hundred foot spiral staircase will take you down to the floor of the main chamber. The oldest human remains in the country have been found here, preserved by the mineral bearing waters. This trip will take about 45 minutes, but you will remember it for years to come.

For the thrill seeker, the rappel tour may be an option to consider. Rappelling is a technique used by mountaineers to descend from sheer overhangs and cliffs. You will be strapped into a harness and you lower yourself into the chamber via ropes. The cavern is large enough to hold the Statue of Liberty and then some. The staff will provide the equipment and instruction, but you must supply your own courage.

Moaning Cavern is located between Murphys and Columbia on Parrotts Ferry Road. Parrotts Ferry Road is between Angels Camp and Murphys off Scenic Highway 4. The cavern is open every day of the year from 10:00am to 5:00pm.

California Caverns at Cave City

California Caverns, first opened in 1850, is California's oldest show cavern. Cave City became a mining town with 20 wood buildings, hundreds of tents, and its own school district. Twenty five thousand ounces of gold had been taken out of the immediate area by 1875. The miners took advantage of the cavern's constant 55° and parts of the cavern were given a wooden floor and used as a ballroom and a church. The cavern, known as Mammoth Cavern, remained a popular tourist attraction until the first part of this century.

Reopened in 1980, California Caverns offers an exciting Trail of Lights Tour. You will walk through the historic Mammoth Cave area and the newly discovered Jungle Room on your 80 minute tour. California Caverns is spectacular in size and in the variety of formations. Entering the Jungle Room for the first time is a breathtaking experience for visitors of all ages.

California Caverns at Cave City is located off Mountain Ranch Road about 10 miles east of Highway 49 in San Andreas. They are open 10:00am to 4:00pm daily from May through October. And weekends only during the month of November.

Boyden Cavern

If the caverns of Calaveras have whetted your appetite for caving, be sure to visit Boyden Cavern in the beautiful and spectacular Kings River Canyon of Sequoia National Forest. Although not really a part of California's Gold Country, this cavern is a must see when you are in the area.

Boyden Cavern was discovered in the late 1800s by a surveying party. Development of the cavern did not take place until the 1940s.

The main passage of Boyden Cavern is 1,000 feet long and inside the cavern are several "rooms" filled with amazing 100,000 year old formations.

Boyden Cavern is located on Highway 180 approximately 70 miles east of Fresno, just outside the boundaries of Kings Canyon National Park.

For additional information, group reservations, or brochures regarding Moaning Cavern, California Caverns, and Boyden Cavern contact 800/225-3764 ext. 211 or 209/736-2708.

Tuolumne Gold Country

Photo from color print by Dick James

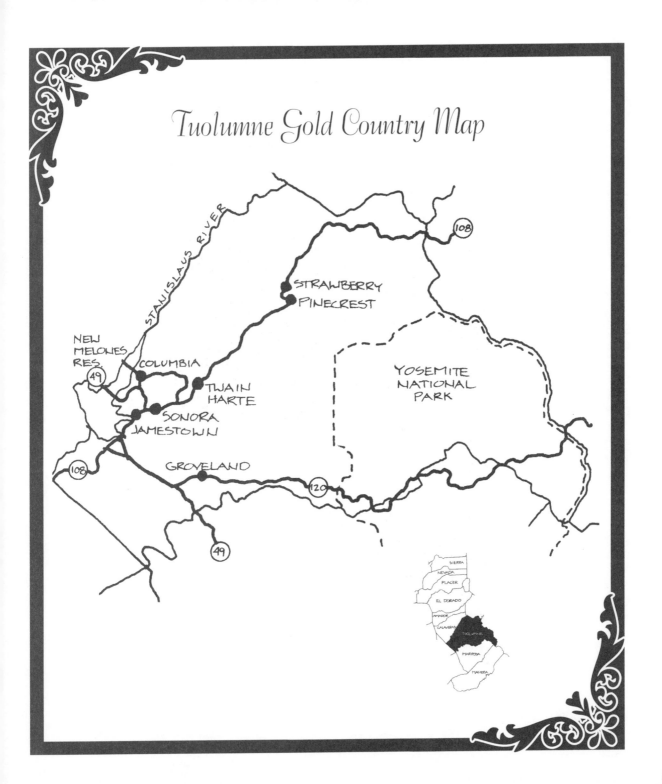

Tuolumne Gold Country Map

STANISLAUS RIVER

108

STRAWBERRY
PINECREST

NEW
MELONES
RES.

49

COLUMBIA

TWAIN
HARTE

SONORA
JAMESTOWN

YOSEMITE
NATIONAL
PARK

108

GROVELAND

120

49

SIERRA
NEVADA
PLACER
EL DORADO
AMADOR
CALAVERAS
TUOLUMNE
MARIPOSA
MADERA

Tuolumne Gold Country

Visitor Information 800/446-1333 209/533-4420

Sonora Queen of the Southern Mines

Sonora has been the county seat of Tuolumne County since 1850. Originally founded by Mexican placer miners, Sonora soon attracted American and European forty niners and became known for its cosmopolitan and ribald atmosphere.

It is said that the campfires on the trail from Stockton were near enough together to show the traveler the way to Sonora.

Although women were fairly scarce in most mining camps, this was certainly not true of Sonora. A large number of the Mexican miners were accompanied by their wives. This attracted other women, particularly from Peru, Chile, and France. Though many were, shall we say "independent business women", many others brought a sense of propriety and civilization which created a bustling town with churches and schools rather than merely a rough mining community. The editor of the Sonora Herald in 1854 wrote "...the presence of woman, virtuous, pure, sympathizing woman, the great controller of public opinion, without whom society is dull and existence is blank". My kind of guy.

Historic Sonora is a wonderful tour for the walker. Thanks to a preservation-minded community, a stroll down Washington Street will take you past many century-old buildings including the "Red Church" St. James Episcopal, one of the oldest (and we think most charming) Protestant churches in California. Galleries, unique shops, coffeehouses and eateries line both sides of this historic street.

Columbia Gem of the Southern Mines

In 1850, the population of Columbia was up to 5,000 and it soon became one of the largest settlements in California with 20,000 residents, 50 saloons, 159 gaming halls, and 3 churches.

By the early 1870s, an estimated $87,000,000 in gold had been taken out of Columbia's top soil. That was when 8 figures was considered a bunch of bucks.

In 1940, the State of California began to restore the area's 1850 appearance. Columbia became Columbia State Historical Park in 1945 and today will easily provide you and your family with a day's worth of entertainment. Visit the old firehouse, a frontier dentist's office, a chinese herbalist's store front, and a miner's cabin. Then take a stagecoach ride or a mine tour. A must do is the pressing of one's nose on the front window of Nelson's Candy Kitchen. Mmmm, I can see it now.

The beautifully restored Fallon House Theater has an enchanting ice cream counter and is where Columbia Repertory Theater performs weekly.

Jamestown

Originally named American Camp, folks changed the name to Jamestown, but locals refer to it as Jimtown. It has been estimated that more gold was taken out of Woods Creek than any other stream this size. An amazing seventy five pound nugget was pulled (there is probably a better word for this hernia making effort) from the creek and that's all it took to open the floodgates for miners.

Jimtown continues to have the ambiance of a gold rush town and nuggets are still to be found in Woods Creek. An active commercial open pit mining operation still helps keep the unemployment level down.

The area is a favorite in Hollywood. *High Noon, Butch Cassidy and the Sundance Kid, The Unforgiven, Petticoat Junction, Back To The Future III,* and many other movies have been filmed here.

Train and movie buffs won't want to miss Railtown 1897 Historic Park on the edge of town. The museum has an extensive collection of engines, railroad cars, and memorabilia. You can even take a ride through the foothills on an old steam train and try to recognize trains and scenery from some of your favorite movies.

Groveland

Another gateway to Yosemite, Groveland was founded in 1849 and was a rough and ready gold mining town. In fact, the town's original name was Garrotte, a stark reminder of the hangman's noose.

Today with wooden sidewalks, unique historic buildings, and friendly people, Groveland boasts the charms of small town California amidst the scenery of the Sierra Nevada.

Groveland offers ready access to fishing, hiking, and whitewater rafting. It is only 23 miles from the entrance to Yosemite National Park and Pine Mountain Lake is 5 minutes away.

Beans, Beans the Magical "Fruit"

Spicy Garbanzo Bean Dip

1 cup cooked or canned garbanzo beans, drained and rinsed
1 T. lemon juice
3 cloves garlic
¼ tsp. dried red peppers
water if necessary for moistness
Blend until smooth. Serve with oven baked wheat flour tortilla chips*.

*Cut whole wheat tortillas into quarters. Lay flat on cookie sheet. Bake at 300° for 20 minutes. Best you'll ever taste.

Great Vegetable Chili

2 lg. cans cooked pinto beans, drained and rinsed
4 onions, chopped
1 green pepper, chopped
2 stalks celery, sliced
One 16 oz. can tomatoes with juice, chopped
One 6 oz. can tomato paste
1½ T. chili powder
1 tsp. cumin
¼ tsp. cinnamon
¼ tsp. ground coriander
¼ tsp. ground mustard
¼ tsp. ground cardamom, optional

In a large pot mix beans, onions, green pepper, celery, tomatoes, and tomato paste. Cover and cook over medium-low heat for 15 minutes. Stir in spices. Cover and continue to cook for 15 minutes more. The longer these simmer, the better the flavor. Serve in large bowls or sourdough bread bowls and garnish with green chilis or green onions.

Best White Bean Soup

1 cup white beans
8 cups water
1 cup celery, chopped
1 cup carrots, chopped
1 cup onions, chopped
1 T. tomato paste
1 cup small salad macaroni
crushed red peppers
Salt & Pepper

Boil for 1 hour; dump the water; add another 8 cups water and return to boiling.

Simmer beans until soft. Mash some for thickening. Then add celery, onions, carrots, and tomato paste.

Continue to simmer for ½ hour then add macaroni and salt & pepper to taste. Simmer for additional ½ hour. Serve soup in sourdough bread bowls.

The Palm Hotel Bed & Breakfast

PO Box 515 Jamestown, CA 95327
10382 Willow Street Jamestown
800/446-7256 209/984-3429

Conveniently located one block off Main Street in Historic Jamestown is the beautiful Palm Hotel B & B. Our Grand Suite offers a king sized bed, double marble shower, vaulted ceilings and a private balcony. Any of our nine rooms offers a perfect hideaway for that special occasion.

Reminiscent of European Bed & Breakfast hotels, four rooms share a marble shower. Each room is accommodated with a wash basin and offers robes for your convenience. Handicapped room available. We also have air conditioning, TV, and on-premise parking for our guests.

A complimentary full breakfast is served each morning from 8:00am to 10:00am at the old marble soda fountain bar.

Gold Country Apple Crisp (courtesy of June Penrose)

Lightly grease a 6 x 10 baking dish. Layer with 5 to 6 cups of sliced firm apples. Mix together until crumbly:
1 cup flour
1 cup sugar
1 tsp baking powder
¾ tsp. salt
1 unbeaten egg
Sprinkle over apples. Melt 1/3 cup margarine and drizzle over crumbs. Bake for 30 to 40 minutes in a 350° oven.

Freedom
Foods

Frozen Freedom

3 bananas chopped in 1 inch pieces and frozen for at least 2 hours
One 16 oz. can crushed pineapple, unsweetened
1 cup frozen strawberries
Blend until smooth. Freeze for five minutes or until firm again. If you freeze it too long, let it thaw and blend again.

Freedom Burritos

Sauce:

One 4 oz. can green chilies, chopped
1 onion, chopped
1 T. chili powder
½ tsp. ground coriander
One 8oz. can tomato sauce
3½ cups water

2 cloves garlic, crushed
1 tsp. ground cumin
1/8 tsp. cayenne
One 6 oz. can tomato paste

Saute onion and garlic in ½ cup water for 5 minutes. Add chilies and spices. Stir and saute a little longer. Add remaining ingredients; mix well and simmer for 15 minutes. Set aside.

Filling:

1 onion, chopped
1 cup fresh or frozen corn kernels
3 cups zuchinni, chopped
12-15 whole wheat flour tortillas

1 green pepper, chopped
1 tsp. ground cumin
1½ tsp. chili powder

Vegetables can be sauteed before filling, but I prefer the crunch of the fresh uncooked vegetables. Add seasoning.

Assembly:

Spread 1 cup sauce on bottom of large glass baking dish. Place about ½ cup filling down the center of a tortilla. Roll up and place seam side down in baking dish. Continue until done; pour the rest of the sauce over the burritos. Cover and bake at 350° for 30 minutes.

Sourdough—an historic favorite

Along with picks, pans, and an incredible hunger for gold, many miners carried with them from their homes a crock of sourdough starter. Fresh yeast spoiled easily and a sourdough starter could be replenished and shared, assuring a dependable source of hotcakes, biscuits, and bread. Some start-ers have been passed down through the genera-tions.

Ideally, you get a good starter, take good care of it, and use it indefinitely. We've provided you with a recipe for a starter but remember, the older the starter is (meaning the longer it has been used and continuously replenished) the better the flavor.

Sourdough Pancakes

2 cups flour   2 cups water   ½ cup starter

Mix until smooth, cover, and let stand in a warm place overnight.

Beat in 2 tablespoons sugar, 1 teaspoon salt, ½ teaspoon baking powder, 3 tablespoons oil, and two eggs.

Gently fold in ½ teaspoon baking soda mixed with 1 table-spoon water. DO NOT STIR after the baking soda has been added.

Cook on a moderately hot, greased griddle. Serve with maple syrup or fruit preserves.

Sourdough Starter

2 cups all purpose flour
1 tsp. salt
3 T. sugar
1 T. dry yeast
2 cups lukewarm water

Mix ingredients together in a glass or ceramic bowl. Stir with a wooden spoon and cover the bowl with a towel or cheesecloth and place in a warm (85°) place. Stir every eight hours or so and in 2 or 3 days, the starter will be ready to use. At this point either bake with it or refrigerate it.

To use the starter, take out one cup and replenish the remaining starter with one cup of flour and one cup water. A healthy starter needs to be replenished at least once a week.

Remember that the starter is a living thing. It likes to be warm, but it can be refrigerated. You may notice a liquid forming on top of your starter, but this isn't a concern. Simply stir it back into the starter. Should your starter ever turn gray or pink, toss it out and start over.

Sourdough Biscuits

½ cup starter	1 tsp. baking powder
1 cup water	½ tsp. baking soda
2½ cups flour	1 T. oil
¾ tsp. salt	1 T. butter
1 T. sugar	2 T. cornmeal

Mix starter, water and 1 cup flour in a large glass or ceramic bowl. Let stand overnight or eight hours at room temperature.

When ready to make biscuits, stir in the remaining flour, salt, sugar, baking powder, and soda. Turn mixture out on floured board and knead 15 times. Roll out to ½ inch thickness and cut out with biscuit cutter. Dip in oil and melted butter and place on cookie sheet which has been sprinkled with cornmeal. Cover with cloth and set in a warm place for 30-40 minutes. Bake at 375° for 30-35 minutes. Serve immediately.

Sourdough French Bread

1½ cups warm water
1 cup starter
4 cups unsifted bread flour
2 tsp. sugar
2 tsp. salt

Combine in ceramic or glass bowl, cover and leave at room temperature 18 hours or until double in size.

Stir in 1 cup bread flour and ½ teaspoon baking soda. Turn out on floured cloth and knead for ten minutes, adding more flour as needed to prevent sticking.

Shape into a large round loaf and place on cookie sheet which has been lightly greased and sprinkled with cornmeal. Cover with cloth and place in warm spot until it has doubled in size. This will take three or four hours.

Preheat oven to 400°. Just before baking, brush with water and make several slashes across the top with a sharp knife. Place a shallow pan of water in the bottom of the oven and bake the bread for 50 minutes.

Yosemite
Gold Country

Photo from color print by Dick James

Yosemite
Gold Country

Yosemite Gold Country

Visitor Information 209/683-7766

Butterflies and Bad Investments

In spite of the beautiful name, Mariposa (Spanish for butterfly) had a brutal beginning. Home to hostile tribes, the first white man to settle the area was Major James Savage. Major Savage 'married' several women from different tribes, for influence and protection. Quite the diplomat, that Major Savage. Savage was in General Fremont's California Battalion.

John Fremont, the noted explorer, had given his land agent $3,000 in 1847 to purchase property outside Mission San Jose. For reasons lost to the ages, the agent purchased 45,000 acres of Sierra foothills, which included the Mariposa area. Fremont 'extended' his claim farther into the hills, unfortunately into areas already staked by other miners.

Fremont's mining operation was hugely successful but the profits were eaten up with overhead, bad management, and litigation.

In 1863 Fremont sold his holdings and lost most of the proceeds to unwise investments. He died penniless in New York in 1890.

Mariposa is a pretty little town in a wooded valley. It is a quick trip from here to Yosemite National Park and the area sees a lot of traffic.

The local newspaper, the Mariposa Gazette is the oldest newspaper in California, first being published in 1854. The original press is at the Mariposa History Center along with many other exhibits of note. From the Indian tribes to the turn of the century, the History Center successfully blends the many elements of Mariposa history.

Oakhurst

Oakhurst brings us to the end of the Golden Chain (or the beginning if you prefer).

Jump off Highway 49 and head toward Yosemite on Highway 41. A bit of the past survives at the Fresno Flats Historical Park and in the Oakhurst cemetery you will find the burial marker for Lieutenant Skeens who was killed in the first battle of the Mariposa Indian War in 1851.

From the very beginning, Oakhurst had a sense of permanence. Even during the Gold Rush, ranching and farming were just as important as mining.

Pine Rose Inn Bed & Breakfast

PO Box 2341 Oakhurst, CA 93644 · 41703 Road 222 Oakhurst
One hour from Fresno on Highway 41 · 209/642-2800

The Pine Rose Inn Bed & Breakfast is a mountain country inn featuring 3 rooms decorated in European style and 5 cottages.

Enjoy the sweet Sierra mountain air in your home away from home. Each room is completely furnished and they are non smoking.

Some of the rooms have fireplaces. And we even invite pets to stay with you in some of the rooms.

An expanded continental breakfast is served each morning before you head out to enjoy shopping, museums, skiing, fishing, sailing or whatever else is on your vacation agenda.

The facilities lend themselves to weddings, receptions and reunions.

Chilled Caffé Latté is a specialty of Pine Rose Inn. Pour dark roast coffee over ice cubes in a tall glass. Add low fat milk until coffee is a caramel color. Sprinkle with ground cinnamon or add a sprig of mint.

Tamale Pie

Filling:
1 large onion, chopped
1 large red bell pepper, chopped
½ cup frozen or fresh corn kernels
½ pound mushrooms, sliced (optional)
1 small can diced green chilis
1 T. chili powder
½ tsp. cumin
3 cups mashed pinto beans

In large pot sauté onion for 5 minutes in ¼ cup water with ¼ tsp. soy or tamari sauce. Add bell peppers, corn, green chilis, mushrooms, and seasonings; cook on medium heat for 5 minutes. Add beans and heat on low for 10 minutes.

Corn Meal:
1½ cups corn meal or polenta
2½ cups water
1 tsp. chili powder

Mix together in sauce pan. Cook over medium heat, stirring continuously with wire whisk to keep cornmeal from lumping, until mixture is thickened.

Cover non stick 8 x 8 baking dish with ½ cornmeal mixture. Spread bean filling over top. Cover with remainder of cornmeal mixture and bake in 350° oven for 45 minutes. Serve with wedges of orange.

Chateau du Sureau &
Erna's Elderberry House

PO Box 577 Oakhurst, CA. 93644 · 48688 Victoria Lane Oakhurst
20 minutes south of Yosemite National Park on Highway 41
209/683-6860 Fax 209/683-0800

Just twenty miles south of Yosemite National Park, nestled amidst seven and one half acres of Sierra foothill beauty, lies the Estate of the Elderberries - Chateau du Sureau and Erna's Elderberry House Restaurant. Presenting an enchantingly authentic European experience, the Chateau's nine exquisite guest rooms are luxuriously appointed; king sized canopy beds with fluffy goosedowns; wood burning fireplaces; exquisite antiques and tapestries; CD stereo systems; balcony or terrace; and over sized baths full of handpainted French tile, deep soaking tubs, and magnificent views.

The grounds are covered in wildflowers and herbs, with meandering pathways leading to a European swimming pool, and a lovely outdoor chess and checker court.

A full European breakfast is served each morning in the Chateau's sunny dining room, by an impeccable staff who is always friendly and ready to be of service.

Add to all of this a sumptuous six course dinner at Erna's Elderberry House, just steps away, and you have the ingredients for an unforgettable moment in life—a true haven of tranquility—a jewel in the rough of the beguiling Gold Country.

White Chocolate-Lemon Tart

Tart Dough:

1½ cups unbleached flour

1 teaspoon sugar

1/3 cup heavy whipping cream

pinch of salt

½ cup unsalted butter, cold

Method: Blend flour, sugar, and salt together in a large bowl. Cut butter into ½ inch cubes and toss into flour. Blend flour into butter by pressing them between your thumb and fingers. Mixture should resemble a corn meal texture. Add cream and mix with a rubber spatula until it is absorbed. Work the dough gently with your hands. Form dough into a thick disk, dust with flour and roll into a 13 inch circle. Wrap dough around a rolling pin. Unroll over a 10 inch tart form. Lift the edges allowing them to fall to the inside edge of pan thus forming a double edge. Press the double thickness of the dough into the rim of the form, forcing some of it above the top. Move the extra dough out beyond rim and trim with the bottom of your hand while cutting against the rim. Chill for 30 minutes. Preheat oven to 375° and adjust rack to lowest level. Remove tart from refrigerator and line inside of the shell with heavy aluminum foil. Pierce with fork through foil and dough all over the bottom. Bake for approximately 30 minutes until golden brown. Set aside to cool.

White Chocolate-Lemon Mousse:

4 oz. white chocolate, chopped

1 cup of heavy whipping cream

¼ cup fresh lemon juice

2 large eggs

½ cup sugar

Method: Whisk eggs until blended, stir in sugar and lemon juice. Cook in top of a double boiler, stir occasionally until thickened enough to coat the back of a spoon. Remove from heat. Now stir in the white chocolate pieces until melted. Set aside to cool, stirring frequently. Meanwhile, whip cream to firm peaks and chill until needed. Fold cooled lemon-chocolate mixture into whipped cream, spread evenly into baked shell. Chill for 4 hours before serving.

Notes

Notes

Index

Notes

About The Editor

Joyce Mandeville, author of 'Careful Mistakes', a sincere and touching novel about life and a woman's perspective on living it, lives with her husband and two children in Murphys California. She has been a resident of the Calaveras Gold Country since 1988. Joyce developed the idea for "Historic Inns of California's Gold Country Cookbook & Guide" in hopes that her fondness for the area and for fabulous food would strike a spark in those who read it. She hopes that others throughout the world will put California's Gold Country on their travel agenda.

About The Publisher

Greater Success has been in the business of promoting California's Gold Country since 1988. They are the publishers of the Fun Guide, the Food Guide, and the Newcomer's Guide for Calaveras County. Many of the brochures for the historic towns and foothill businesses in Calaveras have been designed and produced by Greater Success. Historic Inns of California's Gold Country Cookbook & Guide is the first general market book they have published, but certainly not destined to be the last.

Susen Foster, owner of Greater Success, is the former Marketing Director for the Calaveras County Chamber of Commerce. She is currently the President of the Murphys Business Association and on the Board of Directors and the Marketing Committee for the Calaveras Lodging & Visitors Association.

Notes

Historic Inns of California's Gold Country
Cookbook & Guide

To order another beautiful copy for yourself or have one shipped directly to a special friend, please complete the following information. If ordering as gifts and having them shipped direct, a gift card will be enclosed with your order.

1. To: _____

Mailing Address: _____

City, State, Zip: _____

From: _____

Mailing Address: _____

City, State, Zip: _____

2. To: _____

Mailing Address: _____

City, State, Zip: _____

From: _____

Mailing Address: _____

City, State, Zip _____

3. To: _____

Mailing Address: _____

City, State, Zip: _____

From: _____

Mailing Address: _____

City, State, Zip: _____

Please send the completed order form and a check or money order payable to Historic Inns for $12.95 plus 7.25% tax and $3.00 Shipping & Handling per BOOK ordered. Total = $16.89 each

Mail to: Historic Inns, Post Office Box 1616, Murphys, CA 95247-1616

Historic Inns of California's Gold Country
Cookbook & Guide

To order another beautiful copy for yourself or have one shipped directly to a special friend, please complete the following information. If ordering as gifts and having them shipped direct, a gift card will be enclosed with your order.

1. To: _____

Mailing Address: _____

City, State, Zip: _____

From: _____

Mailing Address: _____

City, State, Zip: _____

2. To: _____

Mailing Address: _____

City, State, Zip: _____

From: _____

Mailing Address: _____

City, State, Zip _____

3. To: _____

Mailing Address: _____

City, State, Zip: _____

From: _____

Mailing Address: _____

City, State, Zip: _____

Please send the completed order form and a check or money order payable to Historic Inns for $12.95 plus 7.25% tax and $3.00 Shipping & Handling per BOOK ordered. Total = $16.89 each

Mail to: Historic Inns, Post Office Box 1616, Murphys, CA 95247-1616